W9-AHS-244

FACES & PLACES

Images in Appliqué

BY CHARLOTTE WARR ANDERSEN

C&T PUBLISHING

To my grandmother, Charlotte Lee Warr, for passing on to me her name and talent. To my father, Noel Jack Warr, for teaching me the love of knowledge. To my mother, Mary Dufrenne Warr, for imbuing me with skill and caring.

Acknowledgment
Endearing thoughts to my husband, Eskild, and to my children for their patience and support with my quilting obsession. Many thanks to the good people at C&T Publishing for their vital aid in bringing this book to reality. And fondest regards to my patient students who, through the years, have forced me to put these thought processes into words.

© Copyright 1995 Charlotte Warr Andersen
Developmental Editor: Barbara Konzak Kuhn
Technical Editor: Joyce Engels Lytle
Electronic Illustrator: Ginny Coull
Hand Illustrator: Lorelei Brede
Cover Designer: Kajun Graphics
Book Designer: Rose Sheifer, Graphic Productions
All photographs courtesy the individual artists unless otherwise noted.

All rights reserved. No part of this work covered by the copyright hereon may be reproduced or used in any form or by any means—graphic, electronic, or mechanical, including photocopying, recording, taping, or information storage and retrieval systems—without written permission of the publisher.

Library of Congress Cataloging-in-Publication
Andersen, Charlotte Warr
    Faces & Places : images in appliqué/by Charlotte Warr Andersen.
        p. cm.
    Includes bibliographical references.
    ISBN 1-57120-000-2 (pbk.)
    1. Appliqué.   2. Fabric pictures.   3. Quilts. I Title.
TT779.A52 1995   95-30826
746.44'5—dc20   CIP

Color Bars is a registered trademark of EZ International
DMC is a registered trademark of DMC corporation
Fiskars Softouch is a registered trademark of Fiskars, Inc.
Fray Check is a registered trademark of the Sewing Notions Division of Risdon Corporation
Mountain Mist is a registered trademark of Stearns Technical Textiles Company
Pellon and WonderUnder are registered trademarks of
Freudenberg Nonwovens, Pellon Division
Plexiglas is a registered trademark of Rohm & Haas Company
Procion Fiber Reactive Dyes is a registered trademark of
Imperial Chemical Industries, Ltd.
Rubbermaid is a registered trademark of the 3M Corporation
Thermore is a registered trademark of Hobbs Bonded Fibers

Published by C&T Publishing
P.O. Box 1456
Lafayette, California 94549

Printed in Hong Kong
10 9 8 7 6 5 4 3 2 1

TABLE OF CONTENTS

FOREWORD

Quilts are perhaps the quintessential American folk art. Though not an exclusive American creation, they have nonetheless reached their greatest flowering in this nation. Originally quilts developed as a thrifty use of fabric. But materials, quilting techniques, fabric piecing, and functionality as bed covers combined to give quilts artistic parameters. American quilting today is undergoing major changes. Quilts have been moving to walls and displayed as works of art. The cannon of patterns is exploding with new forms. There is a tendency to see these changes as totally disconnecting quilting from its rich traditional past. But it seems to me that what we are seeing are some amazing continuities. For example, piecing small pieces of fabric together continues. Quilting the sandwich of bottom, batt, and top continues. An interest in expressing ideas about the lives and concerns of the quilter continues. A willingness to share quilting ideas with other quilters continues the social dimension of quilting. The rise of the pictorial quilt expands, but there are certainly precedents for a pictorial tradition in the past even if the scale has been increased in contemporary quilts. Quilting has the potential of calling the contemporary art world back to its roots of mastered artistic techniques and connections with an appreciative audience. Quilters tend to be a gregarious lot. They share quilting patterns like they share recipes for their favorite dishes of food. They frequently work together on the quilting. They have quilting magazines, newsletters, books, quilt guilds, and workshops where new ideas are shared. This book shares some new directions in pictorial appliqué. The author, an award-winning artist in the area of narrative appliqué, unabashedly emphasizes quilting as art to hang on the wall rather than to keep you warm at night. Charlotte's openness in discussing techniques puts this work firmly in the social tradition of American quilting with the exploration of some very innovative new directions. And finally, there are the basic materials and techniques of piecing and quilting that tie even these new forms into the centuries old tradition of perhaps America's best loved art form.

—Richard G. Oman, Senior Curator, Museum of Church History and Art, Salt Lake City, Utah

"Values drench art with power."

Henry Glassie

4

INTRODUCTION

The old adage goes, Why does a man [or woman] climb the mountain?, the answer being, Because it's there! I paint pictures, but not in the traditional sense—the way that makes sense. I choose to paint my pictures using fabric, needle, and thread, and it is by no means a short or easy process. The challenge for me is to see if I can make a reasonable facsimile of something that exists in the real (or imagined) world and do it with my chosen fiber medium. I want these paintings to have depth and dimension, a good quality of light and dark, and a manageable amount of detail—all the things that make a realistic or representational piece of art come alive.

Quilting was something I had dabbled in for a while, me being the craft-loving person that I am, and I originally worked using the techniques my mother had taught me. For some reason it took me a long time to realize the artistic possibilities inherent in needle and fabric. The realization that a quilt could be an art form finally imbedded itself in my head. A transition was made from thinking that I had to be an artist using paint and canvas to the fact that I could be an artist with needle and fabric. I decided to dedicate myself to making one-of-a-kind, pictorial quilts.

Not long after my becoming a dedicated quilter the competition for the first Great American Quilt contest in honor of the Statue of Liberty Centennial was announced. It was something in which I knew I had to participate. That contest was the springboard for the development of the techniques described in this book. The techniques contained in these pages are not easy or speedy methods but they are attainable as evidenced by several quilts shown that were made by virtual novices. For most experienced quilters the progression of steps will seem strange and foreign because it is different from how they have been taught to work. In class I tell my students that given enough time the "light will dawn." After trying several layers with perhaps puzzled expressions on their faces and repeated exhortations from me of "Trust me!," I can almost see the light bulbs turn on over their heads as recognition of the logic of the process arrives. I believe the primary force for accomplishment of the techniques related in this book is the desire to learn.

I firmly believe in the statement "Quilts are art." These products of our hands contain all the elements innate to the artistic process. My brief enrollment as an art major hardly gives me the right to pass judgment on the artistic merits of any work, but being an artist is not limited by the choice one makes of a medium. I suppose this is why I love pictorial quilts. A picture is a slice of life. It is virtually impossible to have a picture that does not stir some sort of sentiment: joy or sorrow, being noble or playful, something heart-wrenching or uplifting, amusement or even silliness. This book is to be used as an aid to bring your slices of life from your brain to your hand and then to the surface of your quilt. I wish you joy in this journey from your mind's eye to the reality of a tactile creation.

—Charlotte Warr Andersen

SPACIOUS SKIES, 1986, 72" x 72", Charlotte Warr Andersen.
(Photo: courtesy Museum of American Folk Art)
Second place winner in the Great American Quilt
contest honoring the Statue of Liberty Centennial.

"Imagination is
more important than
knowledge."

Albert Einstein

CHAPTER ONE

DECISIONS, DECISIONS, DECISIONS

This book teaches you the layering techniques you'll need to create pictorial quilts. If you have a glorious idea in mind for a project but need the know how for accomplishment, or if you are an adventurous soul looking for inspiration, or if you are just curious about the methods used, this book guides you through the step-by-step process I use to bring a quilt into being.

Picking a Subject

The first step is always thinking up a concept. Ideas come in two forms: a pictorial vision may just occur to you, or a thought may simmer and build in your brain for some time. Although spontaneous visions are compelling and exciting, my ideas usually come in the second form. They start in simple fashion, and develop additional elements as time goes by. I compose quilts in my head while I'm working on other projects; I find the time I spend in the actual process of quilting requires very little thought. I pass these hours dreaming of my next project: picking out elements, coloring them in, adding subtle detail. I have a good mental image of my future work when I finish the current quilt.

The subject matter for pictorial quilts is unconfined. What you can portray is even more limitless than what a photographer can reveal. You have the freedom to "paint" as a painter does, but with fabric as your medium. (Fabric is a more restrictive medium than paint, but only when dealing with small details.) Fantasy and imagination come into play. You can portray your house and the garden surrounding it, or, if you're like me and you have a really pathetic garden, you can use your artistic license to create the garden of which you've always dreamed. Perhaps you had an unforgettable Hawaiian vacation that you want to commemorate in a quilt. Maybe you've always wanted to make a fabric portrait of yourself or a loved one. You may want to create phantasmagorical creatures or combine realism and abstractions or appliqué figures with pieced designs and patterns. All is conceivable in fabric pictorials.

Before I take pencil to paper, I work out a detailed mental picture of what I want my project to look like. At this point I decide whether to sketch the figures and elements freehand or draw them relying on models or pictures. I must confess that drawing from models doesn't appeal to me. Having someone pose for the amount of time it takes for me to draw what I need has me concerned for the model, so I can't really concentrate on drawing. For me, it is a decided advantage to work from pictures or photographs, and having the right photograph will ease you through the drawing process.

What is the Right Picture?

When I have a project in mind, I also have a good idea of the picture I'll need for the look I want. So I try getting the right picture—the one that most closely fits the vision in my head. My first lifelike appliqué quilt was SPACIOUS SKIES.

I was creating this quilt as an entry in the first Great American Quilt contest in celebration of the Statue of Liberty Centennial. I knew the quilt had to have the Statue as the central figure. I decided a straightforward, uncluttered view of her was the most appropriate. I never realized how difficult it could be to find a plain, straight-on likeness of the Statue of Liberty. I searched every library in Salt Lake City, hunting through books, picture files, and magazines. Most of the images I found either showed her back side or were too small to make out any details.

I decided to go directly to the source. I phoned the Statue of Liberty gift shop in New York City and asked them to send me postcards and posters of Liberty and "charge it!" Fifteen dollars and a week later I received a nifty box full of my requested items. But there wasn't anything in the box that I could use. The photographs were very artistic but only showed silhouettes of Liberty surrounded by wispy clouds or highlighted by stunning fireworks. I was very discouraged and still had no picture of the Statue from which to work.

The next Saturday morning I went grocery shopping. Wheeling my cart down the cereal aisle, I picked up a box of cornflakes and there on the back of the box was the perfect photo of the Statue of Liberty. It was the one I had pictured in my head. It was the *right* picture.

If you work from a photo, the picture you choose should be in focus, portraying your subject in the most flattering manner possible and fit your "vision" of the finished quilt. Though it is possible to use a slightly out-of-focus photo, it does make drawing more difficult, and you want to make things easy on yourself. Apart from having a good quality photograph, there are the following matters to consider.

I believe black and white pictures are slightly easier to use for drawing because the monotone of the picture enhances subtle shading differences. It is easier to determine the line that designates where one shade ends and another begins. If you are working in a monochromatic color scheme, a black and white photo is perfect. However, if you plan to make a red apple you'll need to use a color photo to match the color variations and shades as closely as possible. Remember, I said black and white photos are only slightly easier to work with than color. Lighting is what truly defines how you shade your appliqué.

I like the excitement and challenge of working with color photographs. If the photo is of good quality, it should not be that much harder to delineate and make shade determinations. I also find working with color encourages more detail and complexity.

If you only have a black and white photograph, it doesn't restrict your working in color. Use your imagination to fill in the colors. (If you're as old as I am, think of all the years you spent watching television in black and white while mentally filling in the colors.) Perhaps the colors you pick will not be true to life (maybe purposely so?) but this can be credited to artistic license.

Black and White or Color Pictures?

When you look at an object, such as a red delicious apple, it is basically one color. But influences such as lighting and ripeness cause color variations and shading, which bring the actual number of colors, shades, tints, and hues into the hundreds. In order to portray such an object, you'll need to limit yourself to a manageable number of shades.

BANDON SEA STACKS, 1994, 32" x 37", Esther Jarvis. (Photo: Thomas Anastasion Studio) A shore scene from Bandon, OR, where Esther is planning to move. You can almost see the wind blowing briskly through the trees.

Lighting

When choosing which picture to use, consider the lighting. The possibilities vary from the classic polar bear in a blizzard (which is all white) to the Sahara Desert on a moonless night (which is all black). There are an infinite number of choices in between. Of course, your subject matter will help determine what type of lighting you need. Pick a setting that you can watch easily for a length of time. If there is a gnarled old tree near where you live, observe it, or even better, take photos of it over the next few days. Notice how the time of day will change almost *every* aspect of the scene. Early morning colors can be pale and misty. By mid-morning the colors have possibly brightened a bit, but remain on the cool side, and shadows appear. At noon on a bright day, the colors are at their fullest and the shadows are short or non-existent. The shadows lengthen in the afternoon. At sunset, if you face the west, the tree should be in dark silhouette against a fiery colored sky.

When I was working on SPACIOUS SKIES (page 6), I was able to find several pictures of Mount Rushmore. The pictures showed the monument at different times of day. In the pictures where the full sun glared against the faces of the presidents, you could just see the outline of their features. Others showed the sun directly overhead, where it shadowed most of their faces. I chose one where the sun was shining on them at a 45° angle. Their features showed nicely and had a good balance of light and shadow.

Over a course of days the weather will also influence the lighting of a scene. Bright sunny days are, of course, full of shadows and colors. On overcast days, the colors are muted and shadows are not that apparent. Inclement weather will bring rain, hail, sleet and snow which obscures what you are seeing. The wind will give the tree a directional slant. Observe the gnarled tree over the passage of months and you can see the effects of seasonal lighting, as well as physical seasonal changes.

Night and day are flip sides of a coin. Reflect back on the mental image of the Sahara Desert on a moonless night. No sunlight, no moonlight, and no artificial light means that everything is black; your eye sees nothing so there is really nothing to photograph. Add light and it changes everything. If the moon were close to rising, a line of camels could be backlit walking across the top of a dune. A moon overhead could reveal a huddle of nomadic tents and the dunes rippling off into the distance. A remote city would sparkle with tiny lights.

Mountain scene with overcast sky at American Fork Canyon, UT

Glowing harbor at dusk in Faborg, Denmark

Fountain scene with long shadows in France

A not-quite mirror image of Egeskov Castle, Denmark, reflected in water

LUQUET BY THE SEA, 1993, 47" x 39",
Wilbur Fletcher. Made for Wilbur's
friends for their 40th anniversay.
Notice the windows are dark
(which is how windows appear
in daylight).

Now imagine a house or building. During the day you see the surrounding landscape, the exterior walls, the windows. In the daytime the windows are usually dark unless there are blinds or drapes against them or the sun is reflecting off of them.

At night you see very little of the surroundings of a building, but if the lights are on, the windows are almost all that you perceive and they glow with a warm light. An excellent example of this is Suzanne Riggio's TOPOROCK AT DUSK. The sky is blue approaching black, the surrounding foliage is silhouetted, and the windows of this spectacular building shine out at us.

All the aspects of time-of-day, weather, and season will interplay in your landscapes. You can opt for a simple design and ignore light directions and changes. Or you can decide if these variables will be factors in your appliqué. These elements can change the mood, composition, and most of all, the fabric choices in the work.

Working with figures requires a different perspective on lighting. To make a figure dimensionally "pop out" you need a good interchange of light and shadow. I must confess that, even though I'm in my forties, I enjoy watching cartoons. Animation is an art in its own right. In most cartoons, the characters are simply outlined in black and the colors are filled in similar to the shapes in a coloring book. They are very flat looking and that is part of their non-reality.

However, I have noticed that some of these simply drawn characters, mainly in close-up shots, have two shades of color with no black lines between them. Even with two shades these characters gain dimension, and you see light and shadow falling when a light source is revealed.

Figures lit from different angles will change the whole mood of your project. A face posed in a restive position can, in turn, look open and friendly, temperamental, hostile, or sinister depending on the angle of the light source.

TOPOROCK AT DUSK, 1992, 49" x 47½", Suzanne M. Riggio.
(Photo: R. Walker, courtesy American Quilter's Society)
Suzanne obtained permission from Henry Elden, the architect
of this magnificent building, to use a photograph from his
brochure to make this stunning quilt.

Lit from underneath

Low light causes shadows

Side lighting creates
sharp angles

Not enough shadow

Side lighting

Side lighting creates shadows

Lit from the front

Lit fully from the front

I had my photographer take pictures of my niece, Samantha, and my daughter, Aubry, to see what types of lighting are desirable and not so desirable. None of the photos of Samantha are ones I would care to use. Although they may be quality photos, they do not work well when converting the image to appliqué.

The first photo of Samantha is a totally unattractive shot. The light source coming from underneath creates a very uncomplimentary shape across the tip of her nose that would be particularly ugly if it were portrayed in fabric.

The second photo is too dark and the actual shape of her face is lost in shadow. Side lighting is what I usually like in a photo but the light and dark are too defined in the third photo; the lighting causes very sharp angles on her face and there are no real middle values.

The fourth photo is a very complimentary photo but does not have enough shadow to make it a good prospect for appliqué.

For the series of Aubry, I had the photographer bring the light source slowly around Aubry's head. In the first photo less than half of her face is well lit while the rest is in shadow. In the second photo a little light is hitting her left cheek and her left eye is indistinguishable.

The third photo reveals more of her face, and several shades of flesh tones can be seen.

In the last photo her face is fully lit with the only real shadows being at her chin, the bottom of her nose, and around the eyes. Of these four photos I would choose to work from the third.

By the way, I paid my photographer a substantial amount for these photos. I decided afterward that I could probably have achieved similar results at home working with lamps and high-speed film. What I learned from this is that flash photography is not the best method to get a workable photo. Flashes usually are set up on your camera so you get a fully front lit subject when you take a photo with a flash.

A single light source creates more distinct shadows, as will direct sunlight. A truly bright light can reduce a figure to white and black. Diffused sunlight or multiple lights will soften shadows or eliminate shadows altogether. My shaded appliqué has four to five shades in each color set. In most cases, you don't

AMY'S PORTRAIT, 1991, 23" x 29", Kathleen Levesque. (Photo: Thomas Anastasion Studio) In class, students often pull pictures from their wallets to work with, rather than the more elaborate photos they brought. This is one of those cases—Kathleen captured the sweetness of Amy as a young child.

Using Other People's Art Work: Copyright, Public Domain, and Fair Use

Quiltmaking, by its nature, is a traditional craft that has a history of sharing and exchanging ideas. In earlier decades and centuries, the block patterns and appliqué designs were passed from one person to the next without much thought of rights or credits. There is very little of the established quilting legacy that we can attribute to any one person. Few quilters sought copyrights for their work. However, in the past 20 years the face of quiltmaking has changed, for better or worse I will not say. As books have been published, new techniques devised, and innovative products patented, quiltmaking has arrived into the world of "big business"...there is money to be made and reputations to be founded. Many quilters have become professionals. Knowledge of business and art law may become a necessity for you.

DESCENDING VISIONS, 1992, 46" x 62" Dawn E. Amos. (Photo: C.R. Lynch, courtesy American Quilter's Society) Awarded Best Wall Quilt 1992 at the AQS show. Dawn hand dyes most of the fabrics for her quilts. She says being able to dye fabrics provides unlimited numbers of colors and shades.

want the extreme of predominantly white or black, but do choose a photo where the shadows are varied and dark enough where one shade is separate from the next. Shadows give a two-dimensional image a look of depth. Dramatically lit photos give your project much more character and distinction, and also help determine where to draw the appliqué lines.

Sometimes you may have several photos to use for reference. I have used one photo for a background and another for the human figure in it. You may want to combine figures from several photos into one pictorial quilt. You may want to make a composite person from many photos of the same person or use a combination of different people. Dawn Amos works this way when creating the faces in her Native American theme quilts. She may use a nose from one picture, or an ear or eye from another, and then combine them into one face. Dawn points out that using many photographs makes it difficult because the light sources in all the pictures need to be coming from approximately the same direction.

THE GARDEN, 1991, 71" x 85", Dawn E. Amos.
(Photo: DSI Studios, courtesy American Quilter's
Society) Based on a well-recognized painting by
Albrecht Dürer. Dawn spent many hours drawing
the figure, and changing the rocks and background
to get them just right.

LOOKING BACK ON BROKEN
PROMISES, 1989,
53" x 38", Dawn E. Amos.
(Photo: DSI Studios, courtesy
American Quilter's Society)
Awarded Best Wall Quilt 1989
at the AQS show. Dawn tries to
give the beholder an impression
of the Native American
viewpoint.

13

I have been discussing copyright laws in my classes for several years. I toss back and forth information with my students that we learned first hand, or second, third, or fourth hand—in other words, mostly hearsay. While writing this book, I decided it was time to get properly informed about copyrights, not only to protect my own rights, but to be sure I was not infringing on the rights of others. As artists (or even if you think of yourself as a hobbyist), this is a subject we need to educate ourselves about. My purpose in writing this discussion of copyright is not to create the definitive treatise on using other people's work in your artistic endeavors (the legal term for this is appropriation)—I am strictly a layman when it comes to the law and knowledge of it—but to inform you that you should also be concerned about this and to encourage you to educate yourself in these matters.

Copyright laws were not meant to place harsh restrictions on all creative endeavors, but to encourage the trading and exchange of ideas and concepts in order to stimulate more original ideas and concepts. This only makes sense: if someone has created something wonderful, and thinks the concept will be borrowed or stolen by someone else who will not give them credit or reward for their effort (or without incurring penalty or punishment), the inclination will be to secrete the creation for themselves. Copyright protection gives authors/artists incentive to share their work with fellow beings for the benefit and enlightenment of humankind.

Photographs are copyrightable entities. As explained in *A Practical Guide to Copyrights and Trademarks* by Frank H. Andorka, "Copyright protection exists when any original work of authorship is 'fixed in any tangible medium of expression.' When a newspaper article or column is typed on a sheet of paper or into a word processor; when a television news program is videotaped; when a singer's performance is recorded on a phonograph record, a tape, or a compact disc; when a photograph is fixed on a roll of film—in each case the copyright protection automatically exists. The author of the work is protected against unauthorized copying from the moment of fixation." (Note: Fixation and tangible are important words here. Ideas are not copyrightable [though perhaps a patent maybe obtained]. So if I were to tell you the concept for my next quilt and you were to hurry and make the quilt before I did, I would not be able to have a copyright infringement claim against you. Still, I would consider this ethically wrong.)

I must confess to having had a cavalier attitude toward photographs in the past. Photography seemed to be too easy to be an art form. After all, the subject matter of photographs is "just there" waiting for someone with a camera, with their "magic box" so to speak, to capture the image. And since these things are there waiting for anyone who comes along to take their picture, why shouldn't we, in turn, be able to make use of their photos? Obviously not everyone could be there with a camera at JFK's assassination, or there to witness the devastation in Rwanda, or there to take the perfect portrait of one's favorite movie star. It didn't take me long to understand what was wrong with my attitude.

Anyone who has attempted to do anything beyond the most amateurish photography realizes that it is not easy. There are so many factors involved in taking a photo that is worthy of being published that it takes whole books to list them. (Check out how many books there are on photography on the shelves of your local library!) Some basic things that photography entails are opportunity, being able to be at a place; timing, being there at the right moment; equipment (you could mortgage your house and still not have enough); the knowledge to use the equipment properly; and mostly, the ability to "see." As Patricia Caulfield (*Artnews*, Jan 1981, p.17) states, "The ability to see is part of the photographer's art as well as the painter's."

In our past classroom discussions of copyright we have bandied about terms like fair use, public domain, derivative work, and the presence of the © or copyright notice on a designated work. I will attempt to explain a little about these. These are the briefest of descriptions; I advise further reading in this subject.

Fair Use: This is a term used to apply to usages that would not be judged to be copyright infringements. According to *The Copyright Book* by William S. Strong, "A use is most likely to be considered permissible if the resulting work does not exploit the commercial value of the original." Generally, it has been decided that if you make use of someone else's creation but have done it for your own private ends without expectation of profiting from it, it is fair use. So, if you are making a quilt to hang in your own home, or a gift for a friend or relative it is a fair use if you employ a photo you find in a magazine, newspaper, book, or other source outside your own photo album. However, if you decide to hang your quilt at a show and someone takes a picture of it which ends up in a publication, or, if your friend or relative decides your quilt is a wonderful design and makes and distributes greeting cards with the image of your quilt on them, you may have problems down the road. Another statement from *A Practical Guide to Copyrights & Trademarks* that may make you hesitate to use a photo is, "A number of courts have stated that it is not possible for a use to be fair if the copyright owner's entire work is appropriated. Thus copying a complete copyrighted poem or cartoon or photograph, particularly for commercial purposes, will not be considered a fair use."

Public Domain: A work is determined to be in the public domain if it has no copyright or the copyright has expired. Also, works by employees of, and property of, the United States government are considered public domain because we all, as taxpayers, contribute to their creation. Going back again to SPACIOUS SKIES (page 6), all of the monuments, public edifices, and happenings I portrayed in the quilt are in the public domain. All were commissioned by or gifts to the American people. Also, according to *The ABC of Copyright*, "One universal limit to copyright protection permits the reproduction of works of art, monuments and buildings permanently located in public places without the author's permission. Justification for this exception is the publicity these works receive." Determining the existence of a copyright or resolving if a copyright has expired requires the knowledge of when varying copyright laws took effect. Major laws are the Copyright Act of 1909, the Copyright Revision Act of 1976, the Buenos Aires Convention, and the Berne Convention Act. After reading several books on the subject, I have an inkling of how to determine if a copyright has expired, but I can't say I'm

DREAMCHILD, 1994, 41" x 50",
Carol Spalding. (Photo: Thomas Anastasion Studio)
Inspired by the cover of a Miles Kimball catalog,
Carol obtained permission from the company for
the reproduction of the quilt in this book. Therefore,
this is a derivative work.

too sure about it. The duration of a copyright depends on the year and under which Act it was created. The 1976 Act extended the copyrights of many works created under the 1909 Act. Generally, a copyright lasts the life of the author/artist plus 50 years. Many older works under the 1909 Act had a life of 75 years. It *may* be safe to presume that if a work has a copyright date that is today's date minus 75 years, it is in the public domain. But, as the books I read exhorted many times, when in doubt, consult a lawyer.

Derivative Work: This is a work that is based (in whole or in part) on an earlier work. This means that if you took any creation of another artist on which you relied for reference and used all or part of that creation in a creation of your own, your creation is then a derivative work. The right to create a derivative work or grant permission to do so lies strictly with the copyright owner.

I was told for several years that if you took a copyrighted work and changed it substantially, it became your own. This shows where problems can occur if you listen to too much hearsay. As quoted from the *Artist's Friendly Legal Guide*, "Remember, to prove infringement, you don't have to show that the entire work was copied. If only twenty five percent of your work were copied onto another work, or perhaps even only ten percent, there may still be infringement. Thus all the rumors about changing works ten percent or twenty percent to avoid liability are completely false. However, with less copying, the award of damages may be less." This information is repeated in *The Art Law Primer*, "A collage which incorporates an original painting by an artist along with a copyrighted photograph by another artist very well may constitute an infringement of copyright where permission to utilize the photograph has not

INSTAMATIC PONIES, 1988, 43" x 53", Isolde Sarnecki-Devries.
The Michigan state winner in the second Great American Quilt
contest was inspired by snapshots and negatives of Isolde's
children on the merry-go-round. However, she had her daughter
sit on her rocking horse in a variety of poses to get the right one.

been obtained. Even the incorporation of a well-known detail from one work of art into a second work of art without permission may constitute an infringement."

If you have a photograph or piece of artwork that you would like to use for a quilt, but which is not in the public domain, write to the artist/photographer for permission to make a derivative work. The answer will be either yes or no, and payment for the usage may be required. Chances are the copyright owner will be flattered that you asked.

Copyright Notice: As of March 1, 1989, when the United States became a signing member of the Berne Convention, it is no longer necessary for a copyrightable work to have a copyright notice on it. From *A Practical Guide to Copyrights and Trademarks*, "...use of a copyright notice (a notice identifying the year of the first publication of the work and the owner) is voluntary; copyright protection can no longer be forfeited through publication without notice." Before the Berne Act became valid in the United States all works needed to have a notice to be considered copyrightable. So you might think that any photograph or painting made before 1989 that does not have a copyright notice on it is usable—not so! The Act also provided provisions for works made before 1989 so that protection can be recovered. Also from *A Practical Guide*, "Thus, the absence of a copyright notice on a work published prior to March 1, 1989 does not establish without a question that a work is in the public domain because copyright protection has been forfeited."

As I learn more about copyrights and being an artist, I have made the decision that whenever possible I will take my own photographs to use in my quilts. Now I know that it is monetarily and strategically impossible for me to be at places and events from which I need photos. I will have to rely on other people's work and will make every attempt to do it in a law-abiding manner. A copyright lawsuit is the last thing I want to have to face.

For further recommended reading on the subject of copyright I highly suggest the following books and articles: *The Artist's Friendly Legal Guide* by Conner, Karlen, Perwin, Spatt; *The Art Law Primer* by Pinkerton and Guardalabene; *The Copyright Book* by Strong; *Legal Guide for the Visual Artist* by Crawford; "Art and the Law, Appropriation under the Gun." *Art in America*, June 1992; "When Artists Use Photographs." *Artnews*, Jan 1981.

The books and articles all give good overall information about copyright, with each making points on specific subjects that may not be covered in the others. I strongly encourage you to read the material. They each detail cases of artists making derivative works from photographs and not obtaining permission.

Taking Your Own Photographs

Possibly, if you look through your photo albums or boxes of family pictures, you'll find a photo (perhaps several) that seems to beg to be made into a pictorial quilt. If you, or a close relative, took the picture you don't have to worry about copyright hassles or obtaining permission to use it. You're ready to go. But maybe you have some terrific idea that can't be accomplished with any of the pictures you own...you need to look for something that inspires you. Wherever you happen to be, have a camera with you. You never know when a photo opportunity will arrive. (I always seem to be without my camera when the best occasions are at hand.) Perhaps you will need to compose a scene for that terrific idea of yours. One of my favorite artists, Norman Rockwell, recruited family, friends, neighbors, and strangers to model for

his paintings. I learned when reading about him that at some stage in his career he started photographing everything: models, costumes, props, settings—all chosen to be most authentic to the concept. "As with most artists, the procedure [painting a picture] varies from picture to picture—he may do a whole series of compositional sketches in color or, at the other extreme, simply project a photograph onto a white canvas, draw around the image and start painting."[1]

Having a photo to work from and projecting the desired image is the way I like to work. I was smugly pleased to find that I had at least one technique similar to Rockwell's.

One of the things I might choose to be, were I not a quilter, is a photographer. I am not very good at photography but with time and schooling I could possibly learn to be. Some photographers have been making very imaginative pieces. They manipulate and transcend reality with processes that turn their photos into genuine art. Alas, I take very simple photographs in which I am lucky to have my subjects in focus. They are usually poorly composed since I take a point-and-shoot approach, but usually one, two, or three snaps out of a roll of film have something in them I can use. I take the aspects I want out of these shots, and then combine and manipulate them to get a drawing that pleases me.

Projecting images will be discussed in Chapter Two. This process may influence the type of pictures you want to take. There are various methods for enlarging photos and most of them will be discussed in a later chapter. I have found the easiest and most straightforward method is to use a slide projector and slide. So if you are taking pictures with a quilt project in mind, I recommend that you use slide film in a speed compatible with your subject matter. However, if you happen to have print film in your camera it is not a problem. Your photo lab can make a slide from a print or vice versa for a relatively small fee. Having both a print and a slide at hand can be a big advantage. You can have the print in your hand to refer to as you are drawing, while the slide is being projected.

---

[1] Buechner, Thomas S. *Norman Rockwell, A Sixty Year Perspective.* Catalogue of an Exhibition Organized by Bernard Danenberg Galleries. New York: Harry N. Abrams, Inc., 1972

CAR CRUSHER: A Monster Truck, 1990, 104" x 104", Laura Lee Fritz. (Photo: Thomas Anastasion Studio) Laura says, "The common American is my hero, an unsung survivor of daring, boring, and comic deeds. A sign of our times is this 'toy,' a huge truck of exceptional strength, endurance, and folly. It is the perfect example of many a man's self-vision. This quilt needed to be huge to get this message across."

> "I don't have a photograph, but you can have my footprints. They're upstairs in my socks."
>
> Groucho Marx
> (A Night at the Opera)

How Big?

Once you've decided on your subject matter, you will want to decide on the size you are going to make your quilt. There are several factors that contribute to this decision: What is the purpose of this quilt? Is there a certain space on the wall the quilt needs to fit? Are you entering it in a competition that has specified size requirements? Is this quilt a gift for someone? You may have to consider their wants and needs. How much work do you want to do? A very large quilt will probably take more time and work (not to mention yardage) than a medium-sized quilt or wall hanging, though possibly not as much as you think. The larger the quilt the more detail you can include. I like to accomplish these details with appliqué. I feel that resorting to embroidery is a distraction and I won't use it unless I absolutely have to. Trying to put certain details on a small piece can be tedious if not out-and-out impossible. Think of the different challenges that will come in creating a large, medium, or small quilt. Are you making this quilt for personal satisfaction, for the aesthetic, for Art? The latter is the best reason for making a quilt. In imagining your concept your mind may just intuitively think, "This quilt needs to be this size!" and no other reason is needed.

Preliminary Sketch

Depending on the complexity of your idea, you may want to make a preliminary sketch. I find this is especially helpful when I'm doing a collage or montage or if I plan to incorporate traditional quilt blocks, which I often do. I usually sketch on four-square-to-the-inch graph paper where each square equals one inch of the planned quilt. Doing this assures me that I have a valid idea, that the varying elements hold together, that no one figure or block overwhelms the others unless I plan it that way, and that the work will balance nicely. This sketch does not tell me exactly what it is I am going to do. It usually changes somewhat when I get to the actual drawing, but it shows my intentions and that I'm on the right track.

Once you have all these preliminary decisions (and possibly legalities) out of the way, it is time to get started on the actual project.

"The whole of art
is an appeal to reality
which is not
without us but in
our minds."

Desmond MacCarthy

CHAPTER TWO

ENLARGING PROCEDURES

Full-Size Paper Pattern

To use the methods in this book, a full-size pattern is a must. The pattern shows, in full scale, all the lines and shapes I use to put together my quilt top. If you are making a small quilt or wall hanging, finding paper large enough, without having to seam together pieces of paper, shouldn't be too difficult. Most office supply stores carry type or copy paper that measures 11" x 17", or perhaps 17" x 22". Some copy stores have short rolls two or three feet wide. You may be able to obtain some suitable papers at your art or drafting supply store. They generally have good quality paper (like vellum) in two feet by four feet widths; vellum is also available in a roll. Lightweight and translucent (light shows through) butcher or craft paper works well but avoid heavy or opaque (blocks the light) paper.

Some printers and newspaper publishers sell (or even give away) the end rolls of papers they use in their business. One drawback is that newsprint does not stand up well with use. Magazine paper often has a shiny coat that makes it hard to draw on. However, having the freedom to use one large sheet of paper rather than taping together several smaller sheets is a definite advantage.

Freezer paper is a sturdy, translucent paper that you can use for the projects contained in this book, although I don't cut it out, iron it on, or use it as a template for appliqué as do most quilters. Freezer paper has advantages in that, although it is only 18" wide, it comes in a long, continuous roll. You can overlap the edges of the paper, iron them, and then make a larger piece of paper. It is also fairly translucent.

If you plan to make a lot of quilts, you'll need to have large paper on hand for pattern making. You may be interested in the paper I use called Alpha Numeric Paper (see sources on page 128). Made primarily for manufacturer's clothing patterns, this paper has printed on it, in non-photo blue, the numbers, letters, and symbols spaced evenly to mark off every square inch. The printing is not obtrusive and doesn't distract from your drawing or sketching. It is durable and holds up well to repeated folding, rolling, use, and abuse. The most distinct advantage is that it comes in rolls of 36, 42, 45, 48, 54, 60, and 72 inches (common fabric widths) by 200 yards. I have a roll of the 60" width which accommodates the size of most wall hangings. If I need to make a quilt larger that 60" in width or length, I only have one paper seam to tape together. I take the amount I need off the roll. I use the printed inch marks (quarter yard marks are in bold on the edge of the paper) to measure the amount.

If you are interested in purchasing this paper but don't want the expense of buying a 200 yard roll, consider making a joint purchase with some of your quilting friends. Or perhaps you can persuade your local quilt/fabric store to buy a roll and sell it by the yard.

Drawing

Once you have your paper cut to size and ready, you can begin drawing the pattern. You may want to start sketching, blocking in the shapes and elements, fill in the design details, and then gradually

A SWIM IN THE FISHBOWL, 1991, 56" x 49", Anna Judd-Edwards.
(Photo: Ken Wagner Photography) Voicing wonder at the beauty of the water after a
sailing vacation in the South Pacific, and the importance of keeping the oceans clean,
Anna drew the girl and dolphin from her imagination instead of using a photo.

work the pattern into a definitive line drawing. If you consider yourself a good enough artist, this is perhaps how you should normally proceed. But most people do not consider themselves artists and will say, "I can't draw!" This is not an excuse, and I have solutions for those who feel they can't draw. Some may think of these solutions as "crutches," but even great artists make use of these methods (see Norman Rockwell and Taking Your Own Photography in Chapter One). I myself am capable of drawing my designs freehand from just looking at the photo/model, but am much happier with my work if I use these crutches. They speed up the process and require much less mental effort.

If you are drawing from your imagination, just place your paper on a flat surface and begin sketching away. If you are working from a photo, there are other alternatives but these methods require enlarging your photo to the size you want to see the figures, or elements, in your quilt. Most of these methods involve tracing. Yes, tracing, and anyone can trace. Now, doesn't tracing sound like much less of a challenge than drawing?

How do we make these enlargements? The following methods range from needing little or no equipment to those requiring expensive and/or technologically advanced equipment. Review the methods to find the one that works best for you.

One-to-One Grid Method

This method requires very simple equipment: a pencil, eraser, and ruler, at the least, with the possible addition of gridded template material and graph paper. Anyone who is at all familiar with needlework or craft magazines is well-acquainted with the one-to-one grid method. A scale-size pattern of the project is given with a grid (squares) imposed over it and you are told to enlarge it. For example, the drawing may say one square equals 4" and the drawing may be five squares by six squares (30 squares). This means when you are done enlarging your project it will be 20" x 24". You take your paper and divide it into the thirty 4" squares (five by six) and then redraw the lines contained in each square that correspond to the square on your paper. It works the same way for a simple line drawing as it does for a photograph. Sounds tedious and boring? It is!

I used this method to enlarge my first pattern piece of realistic appliqué: the Statue of Liberty in SPACIOUS SKIES (page 6). I took the picture from the cornflakes box and placed a piece of gridded template material over the top of it. After I determined how big the finished statue needed to be, I transferred the lines from the picture to the paper, one square at a time, and filled in the features, folds, and extremities. It took a lo-o-ong time and wasn't fun, so I can't give this method a high recommendation. But I think you will have to admit that I came up with a perfectly acceptable likeness of the Statue of Liberty. It may be your only alternative if the equipment for the other methods of enlargement is not available to you.

Photographic Means

If you do have the negative of your photograph, or even if you don't, your local film processor or photographic store can make an enlargement for you. If you don't have the negative, one can be made from the photo. (As I mentioned before, a slide can also be made from a photo.) Processors can make enlargements that are very big; however, the bigger it gets the more it will cost you. This can be a very expensive method to get your photo large enough for your appliqué. Once you have your photo large

enough, simply put tracing paper over the top and trace your figures and elements.

Photocopying

Technology was not as advanced when I started doing appliqué over ten years ago. Yes, photocopy machines could enlarge and reduce, but the picture quality was poor and copy sizes were limited. Now the ability of machines to reduce and enlarge has increased and the quality of the copies has been vastly enhanced. Things have definitely improved! To enlarge with self-service copy machines, however, you still need to enlarge in increments. First you need to enlarge your picture, and then you enlarge the enlargement and continue until it is the right size. You will find that the image quality disintegrates as the image enlarges. The lines get fuzzy and they aren't very easy to trace. I have had better luck with color copies. The picture quality stays relatively good

SOUTHWEST OF AMISH, 1994, 58" x 66", Anna Judd-Edwards. (Photo: Ken Wagner Photography) Anna wanted to express her long-standing fascination and appreciation of America's "first peoples," and their art and culture. This figure was drawn from her imagination.

after the enlargement is done. One drawback to this method is that you will probably end up aligning and taping together several sections of the paper copy. Also, color copies can be expensive, but not as much as with photographic enlargements. Once the enlargement is made, place tracing paper over the top and trace over the lines.

Computers

This is the truly expensive method for making enlargements. It can't be done with just your simple, unsophisticated home computer. You need all sorts of items: printers, scanners, software programs. I don't know enough about computers to tell you about all of it. However, I know it really does have possibilities if you have access to the equipment. I believe that you would still end up taping together several printouts if you wanted to do a big enlargement. Then you would trace over the enlargement with tracing paper.

Notice that the last three methods require that you trace the picture onto tracing paper. This is a distinct disadvantage because tracing paper is not durable enough as a pattern for anything but small projects. You would have to trace the lines from the tracing paper onto a paper that would last the course of the project. Some tracing papers are also not very transparent and can obscure some of the details you need to see.

Projector Methods

There are at least three different types of projectors which can be helpful when enlarging your picture. Some projectors have obvious advantages over others; some are more convenient to use, more readily available, or more easily procured. Some project a better likeness and one type of projector does not need a transparency. But having a projected image to trace around is the easiest of the

THE QUILTERS, 1994, 62" x 77", Marlene Brown Woodfield.
(Photo: C. R. Lynch, courtesy American Quilter's Society)
Marlene took a large number of photos of her quilting friends,
selecting different faces, bodies, and postures and then combined
them to make this relevant quilt. She used a photocopier
to make her enlargements.

methods. No tracing paper is needed and the drawing is done directly onto your pattern paper.

Slide Projector: If you have a slide of your subject (or have a slide made) this is the projector you should use. Slide projectors provide clear, sharp images when focused properly (and provided the picture was also taken in focus) and are very flexible when choosing the image size. You can place the projector close to your paper and project an image the size of a snapshot. Or you can project the image all the way across a darkened auditorium and enlarge the picture bigger than any quilt you would ever want to make. But, as with any enlargement, the picture will get fuzzier the farther away you get.

Slide projectors come in many brands and models. Basically, most work the same, but a little knowledge of audio-visual equipment is helpful. If you don't have a projector lurking in the back of a closet that has only been brought out to show the latest vacation slides, you can perhaps borrow one from a friend, neighbor, or relative. (They are more common than you might think!) If your quilt guild conducts a lot of slide show/lectures it may own a slide projector that you might borrow. Audio-visual stores or a local library may rent them for short periods of time. I decided that a slide projector was a necessary piece of quilting equipment and I bought one at a school surplus auction for $75.

Overhead Projector: This is a piece of standard equipment for most offices where visual presentations are made to groups of people. The image is first drawn or printed directly onto a plastic sheet (transparency). You can either trace your picture (if it's large enough to get the detail you want) onto the transparency, or, you can have your picture photocopied onto the transparency. The transparency sheets are usually 8½" x 11" so you may want to increase the size of your picture to fit the transparency. Remember, the overhead projector is capable of enlarging the image but only to a certain size. In most cases, the smaller the image the better because the projector won't focus if it is too close to the wall. If you have the option, make a color transparency instead of a black and white one. While a black and white transparency comes out looking much the same as it would on paper (grainy with indiscernible details), a color transparency comes out looking quite acceptable (although still somewhat grainy). Having color transparencies made costs about the same as color copies.

Overhead projectors also come in many models and types. It's possible that if you know of someone who works in an office or a school where they use an overhead projector, you might be able to borrow it for use. The larger models that have a light source coming from underneath the transparency, instead of those with the light shining down onto a mirrored surface, are more effective.

Opaque Projector: This dinosaur of a machine is making a comeback. Many people do not know what an opaque projector is. It is confused with an overhead projector, I guess because both their names start with "o," but they work in entirely different ways. Whereas an overhead projector requires a transparency, an opaque projector can use any sort of picture, either a snapshot, magazine clipping, or a page that is still in a book. This is a distinct advantage if your photograph is not on a slide. With no transparencies

"It's easier to hide your light under a bushel than to keep your shady side dark."

Helen Rowland,
Reflections of a Bachelor Girl (1990)

to prepare, you just pop your picture inside the machine regardless of the type of material it's printed on. There are three disadvantages to this machine. First, you need a very dark room for projecting since the image tends to be fuzzy. Second, the image can only be projected at a minimum size (but can be made very large indeed), and third it gets very hot inside where you place the picture. I fried a student's photo once and have scorched several library books.

An opaque projector is harder to locate than the other projectors. I purchased mine for $90 from a sign painter. He used it to project his images onto the sides of buildings at night and drew the basic outlines. He then went back during daylight and filled in his painting. Keep checking the classified ads if you want to purchase a used one or try looking at school surplus auctions. The projectors come in different sizes. The older ones are very large and heavy (like mine) but seem to project the clearest image. My machine can project an original photo that is as large as 11" x 11". Perhaps more readily available are the smaller models. Although these models are very portable, they will only hold an original that is 6" x 6" (see sources on page 128).

Using the Projector

Once you have chosen your projector, you'll find that a dark room—the darker the better—is a must. If your room cannot be sealed from sunlight, it's best to wait until night. The opaque projector works best at night. You also need a good drawing surface. Since most projectors sit flat on a

DAD & ME, 1992, 46½" x 63½", Kathy Jevne Clark. (Photo: D. Larsen) When the photo of her father was taken (the photo that motivated her to make this quilt), Kathy was only 2½ years old.

23

table or platform, it's best to project the image onto a wall. The surface that you project your image at should be smooth and flat. A screen will not do since it is not solid enough to draw on. Until my husband constructed my sewing room with just such a wall, I had real problems. All the walls in my house were textured and made drawing miserable.

Some opaque projectors are equipped with a stand that clamps onto a table; these models are made to project down at a surface from above. The machine would be over your head projecting down onto the table on which you are drawing. This type of projector would limit the size you are able to enlarge.

If you wanted to make a really big drawing, you would need a fairly large room because the farther the projector gets away from the surface, the bigger the image will be. When I was drawing the child for NAIAD, I had to make some unique arrangements to accommodate my project. My house is small and I had no single room in which I could project the slide of Sharon, my niece, large enough for the size of my project. I had to place the slide projector on top of a cabinet in my kitchen, aim it down the hallway into the living room and onto my front door which, fortunately, has a smooth flat surface. That is where I taped up the paper and did my drawing.

I have found that in setting up these arrangements it is best to work in a certain order. First, put the picture in the projector. Then aim and focus the image at the surface you are going to draw on. Be sure the projector is level and pointing straight at the surface. If it is slanted upward, the top of the picture will be distorted; if it is pointed downward, the bottom will be distorted. If the image isn't the size you want it to

The photo of the girl on which NAIAD is based. Notice the background is not the same as in the quilt, which is shown on page 49.

be, you will need to move the projector—you can't move the wall! Before I bought my rolling cart, I had to find various stable objects on which to place the projector. Once you have the image in focus and at the size you want it, tape down the paper so the image is centered on it. You are now ready to trace and draw.

Here are a few precautions: Once you have your projector set in the appropriate place, and have started drawing, don't move or bump it until you are done. If the picture is moved it is very unlikely you will be able to realign it to fit the lines you have already drawn. If this does happen, try moving the paper to fit the drawing, rather than moving the projector. Also, as mentioned before, since these projectors use very strong light bulbs they get very hot. It is a good idea to give the projector a rest every five or ten minutes. If the projector has a fan-only setting, use it for a few minutes to cool it off.

I would not advise using any old or irreplaceable photos in an opaque projector. These projectors throw off the most heat and your photos have a good possibility of being ruined. We did some damage to one of my student's photo of her great-grandparents when we were tracing her quilt design, and it was the only photo she had. Have a duplicate made and use that one in the machine instead.

It is also a good idea to tape the photo to the lower surface of the projector or onto a heavy piece of cardboard because the fan in the machine can blow or vibrate the photo out of alignment. And use drafting tape instead of masking tape because it isn't quite as sticky, won't leave as much residue on your photo, and it peels off the paper easier.

She Comes in Colors, 1988, 72" x 48",
Charlotte Warr Andersen.
(Photo: DSI Studios, courtesy American
Quilter's Society) Awarded Best of Show,
Professional, 1990 Houston International
Quilt Festival. I think of this quilt as an
allegory of "today's woman."

Terumah, 1993, 32" x 49",
D. J. Berger. (Photo:
Thomas Anastasion Studio)
D. J. used a portrait taken
at her son Marc's Bar
Mitzvah and superimposed
the image over a Torah,
quilted with Hebrew letters.

MOTHER EARTH BLOWS A KISS, 1992,
24" x 36", Mona Lindsey Gollan.
(Photo: Thomas Anastasion Studio)
Loosely based on a 1909 playbill for
"The Price of Silence," the challenge
in making this quilt came twofold: one
from some of the fabrics and the other
from the theme, "Enduring Earth."

LEGS GO OUT TO VOTE,
1994, 75" x 85", Marjorie
B. Hansen. (Photo:
Thomas Anastasion Studio)
Marjorie is a ballot clerk in
Windham, ME. She took
photos of various legs
while the people were in
the voting booths.

On the Third Day Created He the Earth, 1988,
46" x 64", Virginia Ferrill Piland. (Photo: DSI Studios,
courtesy American Quilter's Society) Virginia gained
inspiration for this quilt from a picture
she saw of a thirteenth century illuminated manuscript.
It is a study in circles: The circle is symbolic of
perfection and eternity.

ISLAND GIRL, 1991, 58" x 48", Linda S. Schmidt.
(Photo: Thomas Anastasion Studio) The figure for
this quilt was made from a snapshot of Linda's
daughter standing by Crater Lake with Wizard
Island in the distance.

MY VANESSA, 1991, 27" x 42", Gloria Lynne Smith.
(Photo: Thomas Anastasion Studio) Using one
of her favorite pictures of her daughter, Gloria
made this lovely portrait.

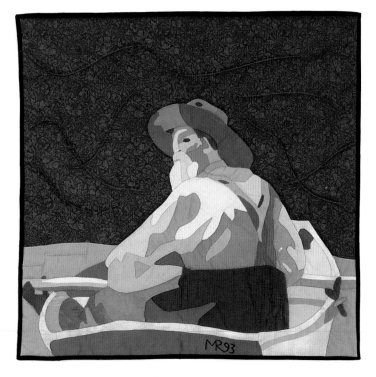

MAN IN BOAT, 1993, 25" x 24",
Maxine Rosenthal. While Winslow Homer
painted his Man in Boat in a very large
scene, Maxine chose to focus on the
figure of the contemplative man.

"The essence
of genius is to
know what to
overlook."
William James

Now that everything is in readiness, it is time to begin drawing. Whether you are drawing freehand, tracing the picture, or using one of the projectors, you are making the patterns for your appliqué. Your goal is to delineate your subject matter so all the aspects of the picture become lines and all those lines connect to form shapes, which can then be duplicated in fabric.

You may have your own preference of drawing equipment, but let me tell you what I use. Since most of my patterns are drawn on a wall, I don't want to have to run back and forth to sharpen a pencil. Naturally, I use a mechanical pencil. Any brand will do as long as it has a .7mm lead. This size of lead can be slightly harder to find than the more common .5mm lead, but I like the .7mm lead because I can draw a broader line with it. I like to shade in my shapes after I've drawn them and this goes faster with the wider lead. Also, I like to have a separate eraser in hand, preferably a white or gum eraser. You can use the pencil's eraser, but I'll guarantee you'll have worn it down to nothing by the time you finish drawing. You find that you change your mind about where lines belong, or you'll see a shape may not have turned out the way you intended and you'll have to erase.

Drawing Faces, Figures, Flora, Fauna, and Objects

Start with an outline of your picture. Mark the lines that show the features of your chosen subject. Generally this is a line around the entire shape whether it be a face, a whole person, an animal, or a flower. Most of the time this outline should be easy to discern. However, in some photos of people a dark shadow on the side of a face will make it difficult to tell where the face ends and the hair or ear begins. This will call for a judgment on your part—you can

CHAPTER THREE

PATTERN DRAWING

either make that shadow, which contains the side of the face, the ear, and the hair, all into one shape on your pattern, or you can approximate what each part actually looks like.

One thing you must consider at all times while you are drawing is just how many of the details in that photo to transfer to your pattern. I always keep in mind the limitations fabric places on me. I know just how small a shape, whether it be point, circle, or narrow channel, I can actually accomplish with appliqué. Part of my personal challenge in making a pictorial quilt is seeing how many of the details I can execute in appliqué by using a blind stitch instead of resorting to embroidery, painting, or inking. The latter processes I consider to be another medium, and I only mix my mediums if I have no other choice.

In order to avoid embroidery, painting, or inking, I do not draw any unattached lines. I stated in the first paragraph of this chapter that "your goal is to delineate your subject matter so that all aspects of the picture become lines and all those lines connect to form shapes, which then can be duplicated in fabric." Unconnected lines are not shapes.

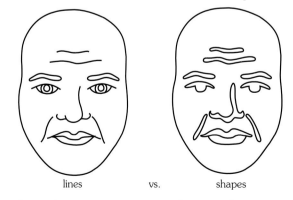

lines   vs.   shapes

In order to portray something with a piece of fabric, you must be able to cut the shape, not a line, out of the fabric. Make sure that all the lines that are drawn connect to form a shape, no matter how amoeba–like that shape may be.

GAVEN (THE GIFT), 1990, 24" diameter,
Charlotte Warr Andersen. (Photo: Borge Andersen &
Associates) Winner of Kjeldsen's Butter Cookie Company's
"Quilt a Modern Day Fairy Tale" contest. The child
portrayed is my daughter, Aubry.

My quilt GAVEN (meaning "the gift" in Danish) was one case where I had to resort to embroidery. I could not seem to draw a shape that gave the impression of a sleepy, dreamy smile on the child's face. I had to apply a slight line of dark gray outline stitching to the corners of her mouth to create a Mona Lisa type smile that looked appropriate.

When drawing an object (face, animal, *etc.*) into an appliqué pattern, the simplest of patterns has no shadows and is made of one shade of fabric per shape. But shadows are needed if any amount of realism is desired. On the other hand, if you look at the shadows in the photo, there will be many shades (an infinite number if you think about it) that are a part of each shadow. You do not want to break these shadows down into too many shapes. But these shades can be blended into each other. With appliqué, the only actual blending that occurs is done with your eye because the seam line creates the definite division between each shade. Draw too many divisions and your pattern will be choppy indeed. This creates

more work than you really need or want to do, and it will not look that attractive. You'll also have difficulty finding enough shades of fabric to use.

For my pattern drawing, I try to limit myself to five shades plus black and/or white, if needed. When I say I limit my shades, it is for each color I am using. For example, if I was creating a man I would draw three to five shades of skin tones, three to five shades for his hair, and three to five shades for his clothing (or for each separate piece of clothing). Black could be used for his eyes (or other appropriate eye color) and white for the whites of his eyes. I believe this number of shades is enough to give a satisfying portrayal in fabric.

Keeping the above factors in mind, let's go through a couple of examples.

Anthony is a white rabbit my family used to own. In the photo he is hunched into a furry ball the way most rabbits seem to like to sit. The photo, while not being dramatically lit, shows enough shadow in his white fur to give definition to the musculature of his

body. The tips of his front feet are missing in the photo, but rabbit feet are not that detailed and can be easily added. I first traced the outline of his body. Since he is a furry creature, I drew small, irregular bumps and jags to hint at his furriness. His ears needed to be separated from his body (why will be discussed later) and I drew a fairly detailed eye (though a simple oval-shaped eye would also suffice). Then, I picked out shadows that delineated his head from the rest of his body, and his front from his hindquarters and the recessed places where his feet were pulled under his body. I couldn't see a tail in the photo but I thought that a tail was a defining characteristic of a rabbit so I added one to his rear end. His ears go from white on the outside edges to pink on the inside leading into his head. I had to decide where that transition took place and drew a line to designate it. I portrayed him in white with three shades of gray, two shades of pink for his ears, and a shade of blue for his eye. Anthony has long whiskers but I would have had to resort to embroidery to portray them so I opted not to and you probably would not have noticed they were missing had I not pointed it out.

Samantha is my sister's daughter and a very beautiful young woman. I thought this photo would be a bit too dark to work from but when

MOTHER WAS A LADY, 1991, 48" x 52", Helen Kelley. (Photo: Thomas Anastasion Studio) Helen loved the ethereal quality of a 1918 photograph of her mother, and duplicated the image in fabric. Since her mother was critically ill for several years, this was Helen's effort to give her youth and loveliness again. Some of the more delicate lines are embroidered.

I projected it I found that I could see enough of the details; it also had a nice amount of light and shadow. One side of her mouth gets lost in the shadow but I found it did not bother me. I drew incomplete shapes for her lips.

Determining Shadow Lines

This is probably the most difficult part of drawing your pattern. Since an exact smooth line is not in the photo for you to trace, you have to make a decision as to where one shade stops and another begins. But there are hints in the photo to help you make these choices. Some shadows are much more definitive than others, such as the areas around an eye where it is recessed into the head. You should draw these types of shadows in first. Places where light flows around a curvature will not be so discernible, such as a forehead or a cheek. This is where it is important to look at the structure of the subject. The light and shadow that play across a curved object define the shape of that object.

Let's go back to the examples of Anthony and Samantha. Though the shadows on Anthony are slight, I could see real separations between his head, neck, and shoulder. The light is coming from above so most of his upper body is white and most of his underside is gray (except for where his feet stick out). Darker gray areas define his legs and the area around his mouth. Samantha is lit from the side so the right side of her face is highlighted and the left is dark. A somewhat curved line divides her face in half. There is a triangular shape on her left cheek that is slightly lit. The smooth curves and highlights define the rounded places of her face whereas the sharp curves and points define the recesses and indentations.

In contrasting the two examples, Samantha has smooth curves and Anthony has very bumpy curves. Anthony's bumps are to indicate his furriness. If I were looking too conscientiously at Samantha's photo I would see a similar bumpiness in the lines. But if I drew those lines Samantha would have a very bumpy

face, looking like she either had a bad case of chicken pox or very wrinkled skin. So with faces I smooth out the long shadow lines and idealize the person.

I thought a good way of illustrating this point would be to photograph two different types of vases: one smooth and one with lots of bumps and protrusions.

The smooth vase shows a fairly even line (except for slight flaws in the pottery) dividing the light side from the dark. You could liken this to the structure of a person's cheek or forehead.

The bumpy vase shows an entirely different terrain. If you were to try to draw one line that separated the light side from the dark it would have jags and wiggles everywhere except the stem of the vase. The bumps create the shapes of dots and crescents where the light hits them, simulating the look of problem skin.

The smooth vase actually has a pattern on one side of it and when the light hits it you can see lines that create a floral design. These lines are actually shapes because they have width. Long narrow shapes like these can be drawn to portray wrinkles, smile lines, or scars.

Detail Limitations

As I stated before, you want to restrict yourself to details that can be accomplished in fabric. Perhaps you do not have a prejudice against embroidery, inking, and painting. These media do have their place. But I think of details in terms of the amount of work I need or want to do. Details are determined by the size of the project you want to do. Most of my pieces are not quite life–size, so I omit many of the minutia (like rabbit claws and whiskers or Samantha's eyelashes and the creases in her lips). Of course, if there are small details you want to do, make your drawing large enough that you can realize those details. If you were making a shark and it was important that you show every wickedly sharp tooth, you would want to make a pattern big enough so each of those teeth would show. Many of my students draw quite small projects (not wanting to do too much work) even though I advise them to make it a bit larger. They go ahead with their plans anyway and amaze me with just how small the details are they can achieve. But doing small intricate things can be as much work as doing a larger project with bigger, easier to handle pieces.

The horse and rider in Sylvia Taylor's HI HO SUNNY are not very large (28" from hoof to hat). She has omitted many details: the rider has only shadows for eyes, nose, mouth, and one piece of fabric makes up his hand (and only one finger is separated). Yet your brain receives the impression of them and you know that this is a man astride a rearing horse.

J. D. Shumway decided she wanted her daughters to have eyelashes, after not including them on her original pattern. To complete MY GIRLS she embroidered the eyelashes and used a tiny spot of white stitching to make the eyes come alive.

HI HO SUNNY, 1994, 45" x 60", Sylvia Taylor. (Photo: Thomas Anastasion Studio) Sylvia's husband, Bob, is pictured on his favorite horse. Her son taught Sunny to rear up on his hind legs, just like in the movies.

MY GIRLS, 24" diameter, J. D. Shumway. (Photo: Thomas Anastasion Studio) J.D. felt she was a true novice at appliqué when she took my class "Appliqué for Realism." Her only experience with appliqué had been stitching a few hearts onto a block. But her results show that you do not have to be an advanced quilter, and, with persistence, you can produce a really artistic piece. J. D. says, "This was truly a labor of love—giving birth to the children was less stressful than parts of the appliqué process."

Simplify Shapes

This could be misconstrued as eliminating details, but it really implies something different. It is more a case of combining details. The best examples I can think of are eyes and hair. Look at the examples in the illustration.

Animal eyes are actually as complex (whites, iris, pupils, eyelashes, eyelids) as a human eye, but the whites of their eyes often do not show. You can portray the eyes with a fairly simple shape if the subject is small in size. For a portrait, I often depict an eye with a fairly simple one-piece shape. If I wish to include the eye whites it is relatively simple to add a somewhat triangular shape to either side. If a truly detailed eye is desired, the individual components of the eye are drawn with eyelashes as a dark strip over the top, with the iris the proper color, and black pupil and whites on either side. (The trick in appliquéing the detailed eye is in the layering process which will be discussed in Chapter Six.) The choice is yours in how intricate you want your work to be. All the examples give the impression of an eye and describe who or what it is.

Hair, on the other hand, is not always a defining characteristic of a person. Hair is made up of thousands of strands, but it is not necessary to portray every individual hair—and why would you want to? I usually draw the general shape of the hair, ignoring wayward strands, and then include some jagged, but not complicated shapes that show highlights and curvature. Where hair joins a face (the hairline), I use the same principle as making the rabbit look furry—a few irregular bumps to indicate hair. If a smooth line were drawn along the hairline it would look like a really bad wig or toupee.

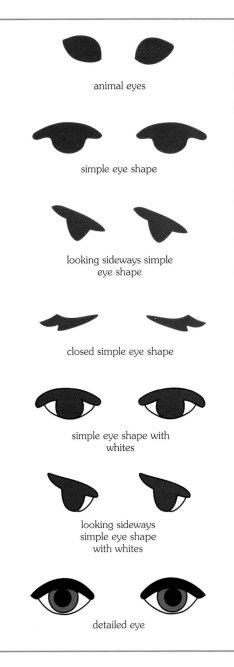

animal eyes

simple eye shape

looking sideways simple
eye shape

closed simple eye shape

simple eye shape with
whites

looking sideways
simple eye shape
with whites

detailed eye

Making the Pattern Layers

Molas are appliquéd pictures and designs created by the San Blas Indians. They involve many layers of fabrics to achieve intricate and colorful fabric art. My layering process is much like creating a mola but I've added a few complications. (Most of the time it will feel like you are doing reverse appliqué. I explain the differences between appliqué and reverse appliqué in Chapter Six.)

Layerability is probably the controlling factor in drawing many of the shapes in my subjects. In my experience, a greater degree of accuracy and integrity can be maintained in a chosen subject if each of the shapes of one color or shade in a workable section of the subject can all be cut from one piece of fabric. This is a difficult concept to put into words as the drawing process has become rather intuitive for me. I will do my best to describe this method.

In any given section of a subject (a section being a face, arm, hair, torso, etc.) there is one color (perhaps with the exception of minor details) with three to five shades of that color giving it dimension. When labeling the shapes for their designated shade, the shapes of the same shade should not adjoin or touch each other. When these shapes are traced onto their corresponding fabric, the entire section is transferred onto one piece of fabric at the same time. If the shapes that are to be made of the same shade touch each other, they cannot be cut from one piece of fabric for the same layer because there is no seam allowance between them to turn under. Adding another piece of that same shade would constitute another layer. (I do make two layers of the same shade occasionally, but I prefer not to do it.)

The illustrated shape does what I call doubling back on itself. If it were an actual strip of fabric or a ribbon, it could loop around like this. But if you are going to appliqué this shape it cannot be done. A seam allowance cannot be cut where the shape goes under itself.

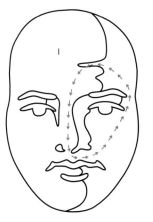

In this illustration we see a simple face that has the same problem of doubling back. If you follow the red arrows around you'll see that shape #1 doubles back on itself. The way this pattern is drawn cannot be accomplished in appliqué. But there are ways to fix this.

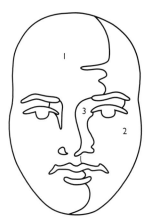

In this illustration a short line has been added so the left side of the face can now become shade #2.

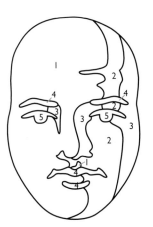

However, this illustration shows a more complex solution which adds more shades and, therefore, more dimension.

PRIMARILY PRIMATES, 1993, 55" x 49", Nancy Brown. (Photo: S. Risedorph) The primates at the San Francisco Zoo were the inspiration for this quilt. Nancy makes animal quilts because "they are important and beautiful parts of this world and deserve to be preserved and celebrated."

BEAUFORD LOVES CHARLIE, 1994, 30" x 30", Nancy Brown. (Photo: Thomas Anastasion Studio) Beauford is her brother's golden retriever and Charlie is her cat; Beauford loves Charlie and follows him everywhere but the feeling isn't mutual.

DARE TO DREAM, 1991, 45" x 54", Jamie Morton. (Photo: courtesy the Museum of Modern Folk Art) Second place winner in the third Great American Quilt contest. As one of my former students, I was very proud of Jamie when she won this honor. Note the beautifully created eyes.

Look at the line drawing for Anthony on the tear-out sheet included with this book. You will observe that on his right ear (the foreshortened one) there is a shape labeled #2 that is touching a shape labeled #2 on his body. His left ear is predominantly #1 and it touches the #1 shape on his head. This means that these shapes cannot be cut from the same piece of fabric on the same layer. In order to create a seamline that divides the ears from the body, the ears are made as separate sections. To create Anthony in fabric the head and body is made in one layering sequence, then the right ear in another layering sequence, and finally the left ear. The separate completed ears are then attached to the complete body.

Shading the Pattern

After completing my line (shape) drawing, I then color in my shades with a pencil. Shading in the pattern gives me a hint of how the fabrics will look when sewn together. Referring often to the photo—this is easy if you're tracing off a projection—I add to the pattern which areas will be which shades. Applying different pressure to the pencil produces different shades. The lightest shade is not colored in (the pattern paper is left white). I first color in the darkest areas such as the eyes, nostrils, or perhaps the shape that separates the lips. Then, between the lightest and darkest shades, I color in two or three more shades, adjusting the pressure for each shade.

When coloring in like this, you are likely to find some shapes that double back on themselves. As you color in a shape you may come back to an area that you have already colored in the same shade.

KYLE'S NEW SLIPPERS, 1992, 36" x 49", Colleen Kane Gard. (Photo: Thomas Anastasion Studio) Working from a photo her sister took, Colleen quilted her nephew Kyle slumped in his chair after a long Christmas Day.

This should indicate to you that you have a problem area. Corrections can still be made at this point.

If shading in the pattern with a pencil doesn't help visualize the end results, you may consider using colored pencils or crayons instead. I have to admit I have little patience for coloring—I am eager to get to the sewing part by now. But if it helps, you should do it. If you have restricted your shading to four to five shades, number them in the sequential order of light to dark— 1 being the uncolored or white shapes on your pattern and 4 or 5 the darkest. Add more numbers or color names if you have more shades.

Try drawing a face from a picture at this point. Ideally, I would have had a photo of someone easily recognizable for you to trace such as Marilyn Monroe. However, that was costwise and legally prohibitive. So I have printed here a picture of my daughter, Aubry. If you are not interested in doing this exercise with Aubry's picture, substitute an 8" x 10" photo of yourself or someone you know. Place some tracing paper over the picture (Aubry's or your own), tape down the

corners and trace around the outlines, shapes, and shadows of the picture using the methods I've described.

You can check to see how your drawing looks as you work by inserting a piece of plain white paper between the tracing paper and the photo. Look closely at all the drawn lines. Are the shapes actually big enough that you could appliqué them? Do any of the shapes of the same shade double back on themselves? Have you made the pattern layerable? If you have traced the picture of Aubry you can turn to the tear-out and see how your drawing compares with mine. If you've done your own picture, you'll just have to decide for yourself how workable your pattern is.

Once all the lines, shapes, and shades are exactly how you want them, go over each line on your pattern with a black, permanent, fine-tip marker. Draw carefully and with a steady hand. Try not to make any mistakes because you cannot use white correctional fluid; these fluids are opaque (light will not show through them), and later you'll be using a light box to transfer the lines to fabric. If you make a mistake, scratch it out with a craft knife. If you have a large project, consider using other colors of fine-tip markers to differentiate between sections. However, I usually stick with black because that is what shows up best on a light box.

Drawing a Landscape

Most of the same processes used in drawing your subject are again utilized in drawing a landscape.

NORTHERN REFLECTION, 1992, 46" x 57½", Ruth Laine Bennett. (Photo: Ken Wagner Photography) A cruise Ruth took to Alaska was the inspiration for this quilt.

However, landscapes can be much more complicated. It comes down to just how much of the details and realities you want to incorporate into your appliqué and each detail means that much more work.

Let's relate creating an appliquéd landscape to painting a landscape with watercolors. I had this experience back in junior high school and it gave me tremendous respect for watercolorists. They have a genuine skill. In the landscapes I painted back then I could not get it through my head that I should use broad strokes with my brush, though my teacher told me repeatedly to loosen up and forget that the peculiarities weren't that important. I insisted on being fussy, trying to get every little minutia. My paintings lost the beauty and fluidity that watercolor paintings should have. I have since applied what I learned to my appliqué, even though I still cannot get the hang of watercolor painting. My shapes are ample, not fussy, with a smattering of detail here and there.

You can really get carried away with drawing a landscape. You may plan to do a lake scene like the one pictured in the photo (above). There are lots and lots of trees in the picture. Each tree has hundreds of thousands of leaves or pine needles on it. The mountains in the distance are rugged and rocky, with fissures of hundreds of ruts and gorges. In order to spend less than a lifetime portraying this particular piece of earth, we need to back away from it and see the generalities of the picture. Only a few of the trees need be

39

depicted individually, and the leafy or needle-like qualities of the tree can be handled and enhanced by a well-chosen print fabric (broad strokes, remember). The mountains are farther away. If we strain we can pick out their details, but much of the detail is lost—atmosphere is interfering with our vision. Forget doing too much detail and, instead, choose an appropriate fabric with a rough, sculptured print.

A great example of a beautifully done landscape is Ruth Laine Bennett's NORTHERN REFLECTION. Hand-dyed fabrics are skillfully used to depict sky and mountains. The limited amount of trees she portrayed is enough to give the impression of a wooded mountain valley. Ruth uses an interesting technique to create her pine trees: She fuses two layers of fabric together and then appliqués the edges down while cutting others into a shape, leaving them hanging to create the shaggy dimension of evergreens.

What about deciduous trees? In the illustration we see a simple tree and a more complex tree. Both line illustrations definitely translate as being a tree, but one gives a greater degree of reality. It would be much easier to appliqué the simple shape. But making a few of the realistic trees in the foreground to overlap trees of the simpler shape is a good solution. Picture leafy fabrics in diverse shades of color, both fading and darkening, in those shapes as you draw your pattern. They will support authenticity.

The bottom line in this pattern-making process is deciding how important that sense of reality is to you and how willing you are to spend the time it takes to do the work. Even though you are tracing from a projected image, your own style will come through because everyone sees things a bit differently. Draw your pattern, eliminate unnecessary details, and refine the shapes into something you can actually appliqué. Label those shapes and tentatively decide what fabrics you intend to use. When the pattern looks the way you want, go over all the lines with a black, fine-tip marker. This is an important step—you will need to see the lines of a pattern through the fabric that's placed on a light box.

Composition

You do not always have to stick with all aspects of the photo. If you feel adventuresome, you may want to make some changes. You might have several photos that you want to combine into one scene. Perhaps you have a figure or an animal that you want to put in a locale other than the one pictured. All is possible. The trick is to forge these individual features into a pleasing arrangement. The chosen shape and size of your quilt will factor into this.

Composition deserves a much longer discussion than I can give in this book. Shape and color and the way they interplay take an integral role in good composition, working on both the senses and emotions. If you've never had any experience with the theories of composition, shape, and color, and you plan to make many pictorial quilts, it would be wise for you to do some reading or take a course from one of your local schools. Joen Wolfrom's book *The Magical Effects of Color* is an excellent source of information on the functions of color and various color schemes.

Paint-By-Number

In essence, when you are drawing this paper pattern, you are creating a paint-by-number pattern which will then be executed in fabric. I would think that most every person at some point in their life (most likely in childhood), has done a paint-by-number painting. If you recall that time, you took the kit out of the box, and there was a prepared canvas with several pots of oil or acrylic paint. The canvas had lines printed all over it. Those lines connected to make shapes and each of those shapes had a number in it that corresponded to one of the pots of paint. You filled in each of those shapes with the appropriate color of paint and, when completed, you would have a painting that looked quite well done. The same principles are used to make a pattern for appliqué. Each shape on your pattern will have a number or code to tell you what color and/or shade of fabric to make that shape. You have only to add a cut-as-you-go seam allowance and appliqué the fabric to create your paint-by-number quilt.

"People who keep
stiff upper lips
find that it's damn
hard to smile."

Judith Guest
Ordinary People (1976)

"The purest and most
thoughtful minds
are those who love
color the most."

John Ruskin

CHAPTER FOUR

FABRIC CHOICES

As with all quilting projects, an intelligent choice of fabrics will enhance your fabric painting. When I began making my pictorial quilts in the early 1980s it was difficult to find the fabrics I wanted. What the fabric stores had on hand were a limited range of solids and lots of cute little calicoes. Today, with dozens of new manufacturers turning out quilting fabrics and noteworthy quilters coming out with their own fabric lines, the selection seems limitless. I only wish the contents of my wallet were as plentiful.

With such an abundance it would seem that it shouldn't be too hard to choose fabrics with which to make a pictorial quilt. There are tricks involved, however, that require lots of comparison and study to achieve the look you want.

Fiber Content

Don't be a purist! I know a lot of you have been told by many of your instructors and fellow quilters that 100% cotton fabrics are the only ones you should use in your quilts. They tell you it's the easiest to use, that they like the way it looks, it

ages nicely, it creates a consistent surface, and the care and laundering are uncomplicated. Well, I agree that cotton is the easiest to use, especially when it comes to appliqué, but many other fabrics are also shapable and have other advantages and qualities as well. I have used almost every kind of fabric (at least of light- to mid-weight varieties) in my quilts and I've only had to replace one. That was because it was of poor quality and I shouldn't have chosen it in the first place. Of course, all of my quilts are meant for hanging on a wall. For bed quilts you would want to pick longer-wearing, washable fabrics. However, if your intentions are to make a pictorial quilt, I venture to say that it is most likely going to be a wall hanging.

WHEELIN' AND DEALIN', 1994, 54" x 69", Betty E. Ives. (Photo: Thomas Anastasion Studio) The government decided Betty's home city of Windsor was to have a casino—the first in Ontario. Windsor is across the bridge from Detroit and is also an automotive city, hence the name for the quilt. The quilt is made with a variety of fabrics.

St. Basil's Cathedral, 1989, 46½" x 62½", Ami Simms. (Photo: Thomas Anastasion Studio) Ami thought this famous landmark looked like a "really quilty" building. She took artistic license with the domes by moving them around. There are over 1,300 pieces of fabric in the quilt—all are hand-dyed cottons except for the lamé and a green color. When people ask how long the quilt took to make, Ami replies, "It took three years and in the meantime I wrote two books and cleaned the oven once."

Cottons

Cottons have several advantages in that they are very manageable and needle almost effortlessly. They have a very pleasing feel to them and with the recent surge in the business of quilting, cottons are very abundant and easy to purchase. They are my fabric of choice if I can find the right color, print, or texture for my purpose. On the negative side, though, cotton is not the longest wearing of fabrics and unless highly treated, it succumbs to sunlight and man-made light (which makes it fade). Some people don't mind the fading and even find it pleasing, but I pick my fabrics to match a color and shade and it always displeases me when a fabric loses its original color because it changes what I have done. Fading is a drawback of painting with fabric.

CUERVO GRANDE, 1990, 46" x 54", Sandra Townsend Donabed. This quilt poses the question, "Are you outside looking in or inside looking out?" Ravens are thought of as sentries and protective symbols. Sandra made use of some polyester blends in this quilt, as well as gold leaf on canvas.

Polyester/Poly-cotton Blends

Polyester really seems to have been stigmatized over the years. It started out as a wonder fiber and then received a negative reputation along the way. My mother was a great lover of the polyester double–knit pantsuits. When they went out of style she claimed it was a conspiracy by the fashion designers. Mom said, "They knew that polyester double knit would wear forever! If nobody's clothes wore out, they wouldn't be buying the new stuff!" I think it was just because the fashions changed like they always do, but Mom was right about one thing: polyester wears very well. Before I got into making nontraditional quilts I made a Weathervane quilt out of Ruby McKim's *101 Patchwork Patterns*. It is made exclusively with poly/

cotton blend fabrics. That quilt has been on my brother's bed for 15 years and it's not because they can't afford to buy a new bedspread. They still love it and the colors are still as bright and beautiful as when I made the quilt.

I have never understood that while quiltmakers (especially purists) encourage longevity and preservation, they look down their noses at polyesters and blends. It seems to me that if we are concerned that our quilts last a very long time, we should be making them out of the materials that last the longest. Polyesters and poly/cotton blends last longer than 100% cotton. Does anyone else see a contradiction here? (OK, I'll get down off my soapbox now.)

Many poly/cotton blends can be mistaken for all-cotton fabrics, but once you've experienced needling them, your fingertips will be able to tell if there is polyester in the cloth. While blends are still malleable for appliqué, they are somewhat resistant to folding (another reason for the popularity of polyester double-knit suits: wrinkle resistance!) and may tend to balk and fray while you are needle-turning.

Pure polyester fabrics come in a stunning array of styles. Some can easily be mistaken for silks. If you want a certain piece of appliqué to shine or shimmer, these fabrics are a perfect choice. Some polyesters are very hard to handle. For example, if the fabric is loosely woven I would advise against using it. If it shimmies and is very unstable, you will probably have to fuse it first.

Silks

I thoroughly enjoy looking at and touching silk fabrics. Even the word "silk" has such positive connotations: luxurious, exotic, indulgent, sensuous. The fabrics are so gorgeous I just can't resist using them in my quilts. Silks come in a vast array of weights, weaves, and textures. Some are very easy to handle and can be just as workable as cottons. Others are very coarse and difficult, and still others are extremely slippery. Each has to be judged according to its workability and whether it can be employed in your appliqué.

As with the 100% pure polyesters, some silk fabrics may have to be fused. Many quilters advocate using a woven fusible interfacing. I prefer lightweight non-woven interfacing such as sheer-weight Pellon®.

SALT LAKE CITY, AWAITING THE WORLD, 1992, 43" x 49", Charlotte Warr Andersen. (Photo: Borge Andersen & Associates) Made as a gift for Tom Welch, President of the Salt Lake City Olympic Bid Committee. Many of the heroes of the 1992 Winter Olympic Games are portrayed in this quilt. It is made with almost every type of fabric including 100% polyesters and silks.

For appliqué work I want to add as little weight as possible to the quilt. Woven interfacing seems to add more bulk and be more resistant to folding, thereby making the needle-turning process more difficult. The sheer non-woven interfacing adds very little bulk, but adequately stabilizes the fabric, making it very easy to handle.

At times, I have even made use of sheer fabrics (ones you can see right through) such as organzas of both silk and polyester. I use these when I want to achieve a translucent effect or change the color of another fabric without resorting to dyeing. Sometimes I use them just because I like the way the fabric looks. Depending on the desired effect, I use the sheer fabric either by itself or fused to a stable fabric. I used sheer fabrics in both manners for the fairy wings in my quilt GAVEN on page 30, and to make the crowd look recessed and in the dark for the Olympic quilt on page 45, and for the transparent cup in the girl's hand in NAIAD on page 49. For GAVEN the sheer, black organza in the fairy's wings gives them substance, yet they still look light, airy, and transparent. One shade of the fairy's hair is made from a sheer lamé fabric with an opalescent gleam to it. That fabric had to be fused to another with WonderUnder® and appliquéed as one fabric. It was difficult to do because the fused fabrics were very stiff, but I made it through the appliqué without any stray lamé threads poking out.

Wool

Most people think of wool as a very heavy fabric that's used to make coats, sweaters, and blankets. However, it does come in a wide assortment of weights and textures. It can be very fine and light-weight aside from being super thick and felt-like. While

CHANGING SEASONS AT TREETOPS, 1994, 48" x 96", Jo Diggs. (Photo: J. Diggs) This quilt was created for a 35th wedding anniversary. The fabrics used are all wool.

you probably don't want to use the heavier weights, light- to mid-weight wools will work nicely in your quilts. And they are surprisingly easy to appliqué. I appliquéd several horses cut from a loosely woven, medium-weight wool onto a coat and had no trouble doing my needle-turn techniques on even the tiniest points. There is nothing wrong with making a whole quilt out of wool and the results can be extremely pleasing. Jo Diggs has made some truly stunning appliquéed wall hangings only from wool.

Lamé

This is the one fabric that quilters seem to really like besides 100% cotton. It must be that certain projects just call for some shine and glitz, and lamé provides just that. It has a metallic sheen like no other fabric. Lamé comes in three readily available types: tricot, tissue, and foil.

Tricot lamé is so named because of the backing on which it is made. A metallic-looking surface is applied to a tricot backing (tricot is a thin, knit backing usually made of nylon) resulting in a plastic-feeling fabric that is very easy to use. It doesn't fray and you can cut very narrow seam allowances. It does not need to be fused with interfacing or to another fabric. Do be careful when ironing though, because it can melt.

Tissue lamé is a woven fabric. The warp threads are made of fine, metallic, ribbon-like fibers and the weft threads are super-fine threads of silk, polyester, or nylon that barely show when woven. (Sometimes the warp is the metallic thread and the weft is made of other fiber.) It is not a sturdy fabric and it frays easily. Therefore, if you are going to appliqué with it, you need to fuse it first. I like the sheer non-woven Pellon® for fusing opaque tissue lamé. For the sheer lamé, I fuse it to another lightweight fabric

DRAGON TEA, 1990, 24" diameter, Lura Schwarz Smith. Made for the "Quilt a Modern Day Fairy Tale" contest, this quilt is loosely based on the book *Tea with the Black Dragon* by R. A. MacAvoy. The foil lamé is perfect for the dragon.

using WonderUnder®. Lamé is very heat sensitive so use great care when selecting the heat setting on your iron. Start with a very low setting and gradually raise the heat. When the lamé starts to crinkle, you know you've got the iron too hot. Too much heat will completely shrivel tissue lamé making it unusable. Some tissue lamés are made with cotton warp threads. This is a much more workable fabric and has the added bonus of being easier to launder.

Foil lamé is similar to tricot lamé. It is usually printed with variegated colors in elaborate prints and textures on an interlock knit background. The background can be any color though most often it is black. This fabric is especially heat sensitive. Too hot an iron will melt the foil away leaving you with only the background. I was hesitant about using it at first because it is a knit fabric and seemed too stretchy. But when it looked to be the most likely choice to make the solid parts of the fairy's wings in GAVEN, I decided to give it a try. It did have a bit more give to it than I was use to, but, with patience, I was able to stitch it down and have it look the way I wanted. Lura Schwarz

Smith also used this type of lamé in her quilt DRAGON TEA. The shiny gold fabric makes a magnificent dragon.

Other Fabrics

There are several other types of fabrics available such as linen, rayon, and acetate. All of the fabrics I have mentioned previously (including cotton, silk, and wool) also come in blended variations. Using any of these fabrics comes down to a judgment on your part. Take into consideration the body or weight of the fabric, how badly it frays or ravels, if the finished quilt needs to be washed or will be dry cleaned only, and if the fabrics will stand up under the amount of wear and tear the quilt will receive.

I have used all of these fabrics in my quilts and most of the time with success. I can't say I like using linen very much because it wrinkles so terribly (of course, I don't like it for my clothing very much either). Rayon, depending on the type of finishing treatment or blend it has, can be difficult to handle. If it

Peacock Paradise, 1989, 62" x 82", Betty E. Ives. (Photo: Thomas Anastasion Studio) Part of the Fabric Gardens exhibit in Tokyo, Japan, the tails of the peacocks in this quilt are made from an unusual piece of flocked curtain lace.

wriggles around too much it may need to be fused. Acetate comes in many varieties ranging from jacquard to satin to taffeta. Some of these are much harder to appliqué than others. My advice for any questionable fabrics you have is to first test them for needle-turning before putting them in the quilt. Don't use them if it seems that they will give you more stress and strain while appliquéing than you need.

Colors and Shades

Painters buy tubes and jars of paint which they can then blend and mix together to get the myriad colors and shades they need. It doesn't work that way with fabric. You can't mix and merge fabric together to get just the proper hue. Therefore, in order for quilters to have any sort of respectable palette, they must collect a variety of fabrics (as much as one can possibly afford or have space to store).

Fabric selection is one of the major undertakings of making a pictorial quilt. The choices made can make or break a project by saving time and effort when filling in detail or capturing mood or lighting effects. Whenever I see a fabric that I feel has good possibilities for depicting pictorial subjects, I buy it to enlarge my palette. When I start a quilt, I go through my collection of fabrics and find many that will be of great use. I always end up going shopping for more, however, just in case there's something out there that might be better for the subject.

Solid Colors

This is your best choice if you are just starting to use multiple shades. It is also an obvious choice for making images that are all one color, have little or no texture, or have smooth, rounded surfaces. I always choose solids for making human faces and skin (though slightly mottled prints of mostly one color are often suitable).

Hopefully, your local quilt/fabric store has a good selection of solid-colored fabrics. It's likely you will have to visit more than one store before finding all the shades you'll need. Ideally you want to find four or more shades of the same color (really a specific color). You wouldn't look for four or more shades of green—you would look for four or more shades of a yellowish, olive green. In my classes, I have students bring in four to six shades of gray for their projects. I do this because I believe grays are the easiest to make shading choices from even though they are relatively hard to find in the stores. Students are always complaining about how difficult it is to find that many shades of gray. Sometimes they bring grays that don't really relate well to each other (like blue-grays with brown-grays or green-grays). Depending on how extreme the difference, this can be problematic or it can be pleasing. For this reason I buy grays whenever I see them if I have any doubt that I haven't bought the color before. I do the same with any color that can be considered a flesh tone since I enjoy portraying people in my quilts. Flesh tones cover a very wide range of colors from barely peach or pink to dark chocolate brown to yellow ocher and burnt sienna; I try to have some of everything on hand. It's great when new fabric companies come out with a line of solids because I know they'll have something I haven't purchased before. I can add to my fabric palette!

Hand-dyed Fabric

The easiest way to obtain several shades of a specific color is to purchase an entire dye run or to dye your own fabric. I have been intrigued by dyeing fabrics and have taken workshops to see if it's something I'd like to do. The workshops were really fun, but I decided that with my small house I couldn't handle all the mess and bother. I would rather just buy the hand-dyed fabrics. But if it is something you enjoy and at which you are very good, dyeing comes in handy for the shaded appliqué techniques.

Another means to get several shades of one color at the same time and at less expense than dye runs is to purchase the Color Bars® fabric by EZ International. The fabric is seven shades of one color (sometimes it shades from one color to another) all printed on a bolt of fabric. You can buy as long of a piece as you want, but all seven shades are printed on the 45" width of fabric allowing only a 6" width of each shade. Depending on the size of the subject, this limits where you can use it.

Some students bring their dye runs to class. Dye runs are several shades of usually six to eight of the same color ranging from light to dark and packaged in one bundle (most often fat quarters). They are very handy because you have all the fabrics you need in one place. However, I must admit I prefer the look of pieces made from fabrics that have been collected here and there. Subtle differences in colors tend to enhance the work and make it look more true-to-life. Take a look at your arm right now and notice that it isn't strictly one color. For example, when choosing flesh tones you may pick a light peach, then the next darker shade might be slightly pinker, and the next darker shade somewhat grayed, and the darkest shade might lean toward brown. These color variations don't happened in a dye run because the colors all come out of the same dye pot with each dye solution being a step weaker with each dye shade. If you are interested in purchasing hand-dyed fabrics, see the source list on page 128.

Print and/or Textured Fabrics

At first, it was very difficult for me to find print fabrics that I thought were useful for my pictorial quilts. They were mostly small calicoes that were very boring and predictable. Now the selection is much larger. You can find huge florals, abstract designs, nature prints, subtle mottles, graphic stripes, homey plaids, art deco borders...the list goes on and on. Today's designers are producing exciting and useful motifs.

NAIAD, 1994, 60" x 60", Charlotte Warr Andersen. (Photo: Borge Andersen & Associates) Best of Show, Small Quilt, at the Houston International Quilt Festival. This quilt makes a subtle statement about environmental concerns.

It is a favorite pastime of mine to go through bolts of fabric to see if they have a painterly quality, what it is they look like, and where I could use them in a quilt. I look for tree leaves and bark, wispy or thunderous clouds, hair for people, fairy wings, or ice and fire—basically, whatever I am trying to portray. I believe if you hunt long and hard enough you will find the right fabric to characterize any chosen subject.

HAVASUPAI (Photo: R. Oman)

My quilt NAIAD took more than three years to make, but I didn't spend all of this time creating it. It took this long to complete because I was looking for the right fabrics: bark and leaf prints, water fabrics, rock and flower prints. I was very patient and waited until I found the fabrics that I was happy with.

Color

When selecting from the various array of prints, there are several things to take into consideration. The first and most important thing to ponder is what color to use for any particular subject. There will be many color choices to make when painting your fabric picture. Tree bark and leaves can be any of a number of colors. Bark, most often thought of as brown, can be white or black. (The cherry trees in my front yard have a purplish gray cast to them.) Green is most often selected for leaves, but flowering plum trees have dark red leaves most of the year. Of course, if you're doing an autumn scene then golds, yellows, oranges, and scarlets are a must.

In creating NAIAD, I was planning on making the water with a brownish cast. I considered the making of this quilt my ultimate exercise in creating a fabric scene that looked as realistic as possible. I looked at water in different places, took pictures, and noticed that most of the water, when standing next to it, is brown. Water reflects its surroundings and there must have been a lot of brown in my environs at that time. I tried to make the water brown, but it just didn't look right. Then a friend, Richard Oman, showed me a photograph he took of a place called Havasupai that is sacred to the Navajo. It is at the bottom of the Grand Canyon and the water is a gorgeous turquoise. Since this is a real place, I could then give myself permission to make the water turquoise and was happy with the results.

Our world is filled with color and, although it is true that the colors available in fabrics are controlled by the industry, chances are you will come across the color you are looking for. If not, you have the option of overdyeing a fabric.

I spent a lot of time (and money) collecting leafy fabrics for NAIAD. When I was ready to make the trees for this quilt, I gathered together the fabric I had bought, but the colors weren't as green as I thought they were. There was too much white showing between the speckles and splatters of green. I ended up overdyeing three different leaf fabrics by throwing them into a pot of green dye. I was very unscientific about it, just having some samples of Procion® dyes around and putting about a teaspoon each of blue and yellow dye into the solution. I ended up with some richly colored green fabrics to create my trees. If you are interested in obtaining more precise results than I did, you might be interested in a book called *Dyeing and Overdyeing of Cotton Fabrics* by Judy Mercer Tescher.

Texture

The easiest way to emulate an object without filling in all the little details with stitching is to find a print that simulates the texture of the object. Fabric designers are constantly coming up with new configurations for their fabric and we are fortunate that many of these new designs copy the textures we see in nature or man-made structures. I am continually on the look-out for these fabrics.

There is never one right answer as to what a fabric looks like. Where I see slushy snow, you may see clouds or Santa Claus beards. I may select a fabric to make a dirt race track and you may think it makes a great basket. I bought a fabric thinking it had great texture for making rocks and ended up giving it to Beth Kennedy to make the baby hippopotamus in her quilt,

LES AMIS (page 117). You can manipulate the illusion of texture in a fabric to suit your needs.

Do not forget to check the wrong side of printed fabrics. I prefer to think of it as the "back side" because many times the "wrong" side turns out to be the "right" fabric for what I want to portray. The back side is often a paler version of the right side. If you make a first line of trees from the right side of the fabric, the back side may be perfect for making similar trees that are seen in the distance. The back side color may be almost solid and of a shade you don't already have, therefore fitting perfectly into a shade sequence. Considering the back side as usable fabric seems to almost double your fabric palette.

The printing on a fabric may create texture, or sometimes the texture may be woven right into the cloth. Damasks and jacquards have interesting floral and geometric patterns incorporated in the weave. Oxford cloth is woven with one color in the warp and another in the weft which makes for interesting color changes when viewed from different angles. Cotton sateen has a smooth, satiny finish that gives the illusion of a slight glow. A twill weave creates subtle ridges in the cloth. Some of these non-traditional weaves may be less stable and ravel more, but I have used most of them at some point in my quiltmaking career.

Scale

In choosing fabrics for their resemblance to an object, you must consider scale or the relative proportion. This is especially important in landscapes. Perspective is the effect of distance on the appearance of objects, so the further away something is the smaller it is. For example, if I planned to make a quilt of an English cottage surrounded by a beautiful garden with a flower bed in the foreground, and then a stretch of lawn, and then another flower bed, I could opt to make every foreground flower in that bed. However, I would probably go out and find a large, splashy floral print with a multitude of colors in it; that print would make a nice, impressionistic garden. For the flower bed close to the cottage, I would choose a small, multi-colored splashy print. The difference in size between the two prints would create the illusion of perspective by having the larger flowers close and the smaller flowers far away.

Sometimes large, floral prints will have the aspects you are looking for printed inside their petals and stems. No one says you have to use that whole flower. Just cut out the parts that emulate what you are portraying and ignore the rest.

When discussing perspective, color comes back into consideration. The atmosphere interferes with what we see in the far distance—objects appear paler

THROUGH THE EYE OF THE CAMERA, 1994, 41" x 36", Eleanor Tracy. (Photo: Thomas Anastasion Studio) A great landscape shot of Death Valley, was the basis for this quilt. Eleanor thought that using the view from inside the camera, with the light meter and focal strip, would make a unique and unusual border.

THE CONTINENTAL, 1990, 18" diameter, Linda Denner. (Photo: Thomas Anastasion Studio) The quilt shows this stylish dance "in motion" with feathers attached to the woman's dress and well-chosen fabrics for the dancers' outfits.

"Sunday is sort of like a piece of bright gold brocade lying in a pile of white muslin weekdays."

Yoshiko Uchida

and more misty. That's why remote trees are washed-out in color. In the dark, objects lose their clarity and become blurred. You could simulate this look by overdyeing or using both the front and back of a fabric.

Embellishments

Beads, buttons, laces, playful charms, and a whole assortment of other gewgaws are available to us. Many quilters put them to good use. I feel that as long as it's a wall hanging then anything goes. Some of these items can really highlight your subject matter.

Pre-treating Fabrics

It is wise to launder your fabrics whenever possible before using them in your quilts. Cottons, silks, and other fabrics can shrink or may contain unstable dyes. Bleeding dyes can be especially problematic in silk, but I have heard of many quilt horror stories caused by cotton fabrics. My friend, Eleanor Tracy, made a wonderful Baltimore Album quilt with hundreds of red berries on it. When she washed the quilt, the red from the berries ran. Eleanor ended up appliquéing slightly larger berries over the areas where the first set of berries bled into the white background.

The dye in silks can be very unstable. Joan Rollins bought a piece of fuchsia-colored silk dupioni (fuch-

sia is an especially difficult color for migration) to incorporate into a quilt she was making. The silk bled terribly. Joan tried every remedy to try to stop the color from bleeding out of the fabric but she never succeeded. Needless to say, she never used the fabric in her quilt.

When in doubt about a fabric color's stability, stitch it to a piece of white fabric and launder them together. If the color bleeds onto the white fabric, you may not want to use that fabric.

I try washing all my fabrics before using them in my quilts, but I confess I haven't been very consistent about it. I may have just bought a fabric and was too impatient or in too big a hurry to launder it. I had been in the habit of washing everything as soon as I bought it, but now I've lapsed into my neglectful ways. When I do manage to get the fabric washed, I usually don't bother ironing it. It gets folded up and put on a shelf where it's bound to get wrinkled anyway. Once I am ready to use it, I do iron it smooth so I can easily trace my appliqué lines onto it.

Many of the fabrics I buy and use, such as silks, rayons, and acetates, are marked dry-clean only. I often ignore this and wash the fabric anyway. Silks are most certainly washable. When manufacturers process the silk fibers into fabric they use boiling water and steam, so washing your silk fabric is not going to hurt it. You may have some textural changes though. If the end bolt of my fabric is marked as dry-clean only, I cut two 2" squares from the fabric. One I leave untouched and the other I wash and iron. Comparing the two swatches, I look for textural changes and shrinkage. If there is a change, it's usually OK. I am typically not unhappy enough with it to discourage me from washing the fabric if I think it is needed. And, theoretically, once all the fabrics have been pretreated, I should be able to wash my quilts without any problems.

Once the fabrics are selected, washed, and ironed, you are ready to transfer your appliqué lines.

A CELEBRATION OF SIGHT: CATARACT SURGERY, 1993, 88" x 64", Suzanne M. Riggio. (Photo: Charles R. Lynch) The panels of the quilt progress from showing sight before surgery, during the recovery, to the vision finally clearing and seeing a view of the lights of Charleston, WV, (Suzanne's home city) through the window. Some of the embellishments on this quilt include rattail braid, eye patches, and glass teardrops.

DASH AWAY ALL, 1993, 80" x 32", Colleen Kane Gard. (Photo: Thomas Anastasion Studio) Inspired by many Christmas collectibles, the quilt has a lot of little doodads on it, such as miniature lights on the house.

*"Art makes no laws—
only very difficult
complicated
suggestions."*

John Gardner

CHAPTER FIVE

TRANSFERRING AND MARKING

Light Box

There are several methods advocated for transferring pattern lines to fabric. Due to the complexity of the processes involved in making pictorial quilts, I feel that using a light box is the only acceptable method for tracing your stitching lines. A light box is simply a flat, clear or translucent surface lit from behind. If I had the space and the money, a large, well-lit drafting table would be the ideal working surface for me.

Making a Light Box

If you or someone you know is handy at carpentry, a light box is a fairly simple item to build. A box can be constructed of wood with fluorescent light fixtures installed inside (you can purchase lights that are ready to plug in—no wiring is required) and then a glass or Plexiglas® is framed or inlaid on top of the box. If you build your own box, make the size large enough for big projects; if portability is desired, take weight and size into consideration.

I made a light box that required very little construction at all. I purchased a large, clear Rubbermaid® storage box with a single ridge that framed the bottom of the box. This ridge measured 11" x 17". My local plastics dealer sold precut Plexiglas in 11" x 17" sheets and I had him nip off the corners of the sheet so it would fit inside the rounded corners of the ridge on the storage box. The local home improvement store sold self-contained fluorescent light fixtures. I found the 12" model fit nicely when placed inside the box. Now, whenever I need a functioning light box, I just invert the box and place the plastic sheet on top and the light fixture on the bottom. It's not as nice as a pre-constructed or commercial box but it will do, and you can load up all your supplies for a workshop into the box and easily carry everything you need.

Alternatives to a Light Box

Items that you may already have can be used as a light box. If you have a sheet of glass, or clear or translucent plastic, you can elevate the glass with four cans (by putting one can under each corner), and then put a light underneath, such as an auto trouble light. Your household furnishings will even suffice for a lighted surface. Perhaps your dining table is the type that has leaves. Simply spread the table apart and put your sheet of glass where the gap is with a light source below. If you have a glass dining or coffee table, just put a lamp underneath and you have a great lit surface. The windows in your house are also great light boxes. The drawbacks being that you have to work vertically (have lots of masking tape on hand) and since the sun is your light source, you are limited to working during the daytime. Very overcast days can be a problem, too. Yet, this is not a bad way to work. I did not have a light box when I made my Liberty quilt, SPACIOUS SKIES (page 6), so I used my kitchen window for transferring all my appliqué lines (though putting up with numb arms is another inconvenience).

A recent addition to my quiltmaking supplies was a 9" x 12" Plexiglas clipboard. I clip or tape a pattern for a small project onto it, place my fabric over the pattern, and hold it over a light source so I have a small, very portable light box. You can find these clipboards at many places that sell office supplies.

Any flat, clear or translucent surface with a light source behind it can be used for marking your lines. The following story illustrates what ingenuity can accomplish: I had a commission for a quilt with a very tight deadline. Many quilt instructors like to take their projects to work on while they are traveling, but I am not one of them. But, this commission left me no choice. I worked on the quilt in the airport, aboard the tiny plane on the way to my teaching venue, and in the hotel after classes instead of socializing with the local quilters as I like to do. At one point I had completed stitching all the sections that I had already marked on the light box at home and I needed to mark some more. Glancing about the hotel room I couldn't see anything that would function as a light box except the window. However, it was at night and I thought of putting a lamp right next to the window and going outside to work since I was on the ground level of the hotel. But as I thought more about it I pictured the hotel security arresting me as a Peeping Tom (Thomasina?) and hauling me off to jail. I was getting rather anxious at this point. There had to be something I could use. I decided to see what I could find outside my room. In the hall, just a few doors down, was a soft-drink machine. It was the type that has the whole front of the machine lit—it made an excellent light box. I taped my pattern and fabric to the front of the machine and traced to my heart's content. Fellow guests walked by and gave me quizzical looks. I just said, "Don't ask."

Using a Light Box

If you've never used a light box before, there is nothing complex about using one. As I noted in the above story, it is just a matter of tracing. Instead of tracing around templates as you traditionally do with appliqué, you trace directly from the pattern. Your full-sized pattern is laid, face up, directly on top of the flat, lit surface. The corners are secured by using masking or drafting tape. Your chosen fabric is then laid on top of the pattern. As with any piecing or appliqué, it is a good idea to iron your fabric nice and flat before you trace. If you have a small light box and a large pattern, you may want to pin your fabric to the pattern so that you can move the section you are tracing over the light source. Then you can simply trace the lines that you need to appliqué the piece.

Perhaps you think this can't be done with dark fabrics because the light won't show through. I have encountered very few fabrics that I can't see my pattern lines through using a good light box. The only type of fabrics that are really difficult to see through are a few busy darker prints, especially ones with metallic printing on them. Even then, if you work slowly and carefully, you will be able to pick out the lines and trace from your pattern to the fabric.

What to Use for Marking

When tracing appliqué lines, care should be used in your choice of markers. Even though you may have used great precision in transferring the lines to your fabric, some inaccuracies are bound to occur. Your hand can waiver a bit and your pattern may be somewhat hard to see through the fabric. As a result the two marking lines will not match up exactly when you match fabric to background. Or you may change your mind about the specific shape while you're appliquéing it down. This is why you need to be sure you have used a marking method that can be totally removed without much effort.

There are many products on the market today made with quilters in mind. Most of them are well-thought-out, dependable products. After trying most of them, the one I am the most comfortable using is the Dixon washout cloth marker. It is a chalk-type marker in a large-barreled wooden shaft. The marker comes in red, blue, and green. You need a double-size barrel pencil sharpener to sharpen it. I recommend getting a metal sharpener to do this as the plastic sharpeners aren't sturdy enough (the blade shimmies and then the point snaps off). Metal pencil sharpeners are available at most art supply stores. The hand-cranked sharpeners with several different sizes of holes also work well for these markers. The chalk markings from Dixon markers wear away eventually, but usually not too soon for the appliqué to be completed. I have projects that have been in process for several years and the markings from these markers are still visible. Usually by the time a project is completed the chalk markings have disappeared. If any remains when the work is done, it can be washed away quite easily. I have tested this marker on several different types of fabrics and I've never had any

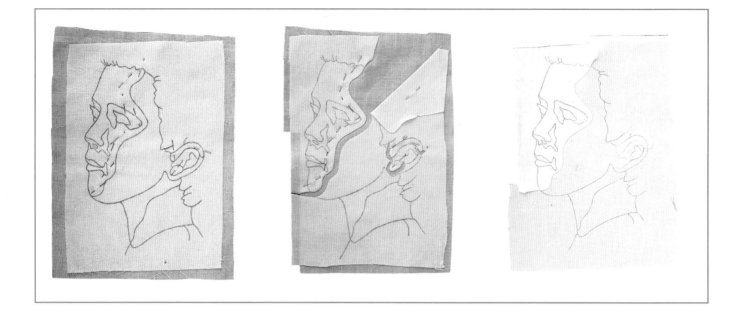

problem removing it from my fabric. Two of my students have told me that they had some trouble getting the red-colored marker out of particular fabrics, but I, personally, have never had trouble with it. I use the Dixon washout cloth markers for all of my appliqué and for marking most of my quilting lines. However, this well-used advice holds true: always test any new product on your fabric to make certain it is removable!

Carol Wagner recently told me of a problem she had with a marker. She also likes using the Dixon washout cloth markers and purchased a blue marking pencil that looks exactly like the Dixon except for the name on the side. Carol thought she was getting the same product, only marketed under a different name, and would get the same results. After using the alternative brand marker, the marks were still present so she laundered the quilt. The marks were still there! Carol said she tried several methods to remove the marks but she could find nothing that would get them out. Be cautious when trying anything new!

One advantage the Dixon markers have for me is that I can use a "heavy hand" with them. I can press fairly hard (don't press too hard or the point will snap off) and get a very visible line. You can't do this with most carbon pencils for fear that you won't be able to get the lines out.

Every once in a while I will come across a fabric that the Dixon markers will not adhere to well. Then I use EZ International's white pencil or Roxanne's Quilter's Choice white pencil. There are a few others I've tried and liked, but I always seem to come back to my favorites.

There are certain markers that I would never consider using. They are fade-away markers that vanish in 24 to 48 hours and the "spit" markers (ones you are supposed to dampen with water and the markings disappear). I have heard many horror stories about these markers. They have felt tips and dispense their "magic" fluids in a fairly broad line. The ink has chemicals in it that makes these markers do what they do, but these chemicals can cause drastic problems as time and atmosphere wear on your quilt fabric. I know several people who use these products, but I do not want to risk the quilts that I have spent months of my life creating to a product which I have any doubts about.

These are my preferences. I know there are other markers that will give satisfactory results, but I haven't had the time or the desire to use them extensively enough to render an informed opinion about them. Someone who has, though, is Dixie Haywood. She wrote a very good article about marking pencils in the Jan/Feb 1994 issue of *Quilter's Newsletter Magazine*. The article is worth reading, so go to the trouble of looking it up.

Grain Lines

When marking your fabrics, you should give a thought to grain line. I like to try to have all my grain lines running in the same direction throughout the

whole collage of appliqué pieces, unless, of course, a fabric has a print or texture which needs to run in a certain direction. Most of my quilts are square or rectangular. In order to get the grain lines all running the same direction, I simply line up the selvages or the grain lines with the edges of the pattern or paper. If I have used the Alpha Numeric Paper (see Chapter Two) to make my pattern, I have the added advantage in that the markings on the paper will show me where to place my grain lines.

What Should Be Marked?

Once you have your marker selected and the light box with pattern and fabric layered on it, you are ready to transfer the appliqué lines to your fabric. If you are making a figure with several shades as described in Chapter Three, you will be using my layering process. This process involves layering from the top down, much the same way as a mola is made. To accomplish this you will need to mark much more of the pattern onto the fabric than if you were using templates. Pick a workable section of the pattern that is shaded for one color such as a face, hair, or arm. Select the lightest of the four to five shades you have elected to use for this section. Trace the whole section—this means all the lines that make up the section—onto the right side of the fabric plus about a ½" of any lines from adjoining sections that connect to the section you are working on. (The extra markings help when aligning and joining other sections.)

No markings are made on the remaining shades of fabric as of yet. One layer is appliquéed, and then the work is realigned on the pattern. The marks or lines that have been removed as a result of the appliqué are redrawn on the second layer. These steps, appliquéing and redrawing, are repeated through each remaining layer. The above photos of NAIAD in progress illustrate the process of marking each succeeding layer. Note how no marking is done on the underneath layer until the top layer has been appliquéd. This layering technique will be explained in detail in Chapter Seven.

If you are making a landscape, you will not be layering from the top down as you would if you were making a shaded figure. Instead you will be layering from the background forward (the background being what in reality would be the very furthest thing from your eye). However, most quilters use a backing muslin to build their pictures on. I do not like doing this because it produces a build-up of layers which will later cause difficulty with quilting.

To avoid a problem with build-up, I trace each shape on the right side of the fabric within a ½" of all adjoining lines, and then cut the shape with generous (about 1") seam allowances. As each piece comes forward toward your eye, it is lapped over the previous piece. The 1" seam allowances give me enough room to pin each succeeding piece to the preceding one. More about this technique will be explained in Chapter Eight.

FROM THE SADDLE, 1993, 39" x 56",
June Jaeger. June often takes
photos from horseback, so this quilt
shows the view of Mt. Hood
from atop her horse Sterling
(note the mane and ears).

YOU'RE PLAYING MY SONG, 1992,
40" x 50", June Jaeger. (Photo:
Thomas Anastasion Studio) A
number of sources were used to
portray this running horse with
its agility and power. June loves
to paint and decided to try
"painting" with fabric.

LA FIESTA DE SANTA FE,
1994, 56" x 70", Carol
Meyer. (Photo: Thomas
Anastasion Studio) Carol
lived in New Mexico for
many years and became
interested in the tri-cultural
influences of the area. This
quilt pays tribute to the
Hispanic culture.

LEGACY OF LOVE, 1994,
41" x 45", Carol Johnson,
Dedicated to the memory
of Kayoko Kinoshita
Johnson: the mother of
the two children depicted
in the quilt. Carol's
daughter-in-law, Kayoko,
died of cancer in 1991.
The quilt expresses the
blending of the East and
West cultures, and
Kayoko's love for her
children.

WINTER WOLF, 1994, 42" x 54", Linda S. Schmidt.
(Photo: Thomas Anastasion Studio) Inspired by a visit
to "wolf heaven" in Washington state. Linda made this
quilt for her son Michael's room. The wolf's eyes
glow out of this quilt in which the artist made
splendid use of the printed fabrics.

"To everything there is a season, and a time to every purpose under the heaven...a time to rend, and a time to sew...."

Ecclesiastes 3:1&7

CHAPTER SIX

NEEDLE-TURN APPLIQUÉ

The Politics of Appliqué

Before getting into my layering techniques, I'd like to go through the basics of needle-turn appliqué. There seems to be very little middle ground in the politics of appliqué. Most quilters either love it or hate it. Perhaps some of the dislike for the process comes from poor or tedious techniques.

It took me a long time in my quilting experiences before I ever tried appliqué. Of course, working in a solitary mode and learning what I knew from magazines did not help. I remember looking at the appliqué instructions and being boggled by them. The instructions showed several steps including marking your shape on the right side of the fabric with a template, cutting out the shape with a ¼" seam allowance, machine stitching on that marking to stay-stitch the fabric, clipping inside curves and points, notching outside curves, basting under the seam allowance, and, finally, appliquéing the shape to your background fabric. It sounded like a tedious and boring process so it's no wonder I had no inclination to try it.

When I finally joined a quilting group and started mingling with other quilters, I found there were several "schools of thought" on appliqué. Everyone had their own theory for the best way to appliqué. It wasn't until I had the opportunity to watch over Jeana Kimball's shoulder as she did her needle-turn appliqué that I realized appliqué didn't need to be the drawn-out and dreary process it had always seemed to me. Jeana marked her shape on the fabric, pinned it in place, used her needle to turn the seam allowance under, and used a blind stitch to secure it to the background. With Jeana's little demonstration, I found myself ready and eager to give appliqué a go. I tried it and I liked it. I quickly grew to love it and found that I had an affinity for it. I believe that to become a card-carrying member of the "I Love Appliqué" party only takes learning the proper techniques.

Equipment

FABRIC: Of course, you need fabric and we've already discussed different fabrics in Chapter Four. Have the pattern already traced on the fabric before you start.

NEEDLES: The needles I use most often for appliqué are 12 sharps. These needles are long, very thin, and very sharp. Thin and sharp is of major importance because when you are stitching the bottom of a clipped piece of fabric, a fat, blunt needle will force apart the individual threads in the fabric and cause fraying. At times I will also use a straw or milliner needle, which is about a ½" longer than the sharps but are still very sharp, though not quite as thin.

THREAD: Thread should be matched in color as closely as possible to the fabric you are appliquéing down. Most quilters will tell you to use only 100% cotton thread. For me, only the matching part is important, so I will use whatever thread I have around that matches my fabric. I don't care if it is the cheap, 100% polyester thread that most quilters turn up their noses at. They tell me it knots too much, but, personally, I do not find that it knots any more than any other thread. I will even tell you that I prefer the cheap thread because it is thinner than the premium threads; therefore my appliqué stitches show less. I've used silk thread and one strand of embroidery floss, but have found they fray more than I would like them

GOSSIP AT BIRDPEEP, 1995, 19" x 8",
Jeana Kimball. (Photo: Thomas Anastasion
Studio) A gathering of sparrows at daybreak
stitched by a master of appliqué. This small piece
was not quilted, but matted and framed instead.

to. I do like DMC machine embroidery thread for appliquéing. If you ever get a chance to look at the thread racks in my sewing room, you'll see that there's a little bit of every type of thread.

PINS: Some people prefer to baste their appliqué pieces in place, but I feel I can get to my stitching quicker if I pin them where they belong. Regular-sized pins can be hazardous since they poke you in the hand when you bunch up your fabric and the threads get hooked around the pins that are sticking out. Someone suggested that I try the ½" sequin pins. They are small and stay out of the way, but they are also terribly hard to handle and they don't stay put. I then tried ¾" extra sharp appliqué pins and found them to be the pins I prefer. They are short, stay out of the way, and they usually don't poke me in the palm of my hand. I still hook my thread around them once in a while, but it doesn't happen as often. However, these pins are very hard to find and Dritz no longer packages them for retail. When you do find the ¾" length, they are usually poor quality with terribly blunt points. I ended up buying them in bulk—20 pounds of them at once. I know of one source for them, which I list in the source list on page 128.

SCISSORS: Good scissors are of essential importance to your work. I use small, fine embroidery scissors that are very sharp and cut all the way to the point. If you are using scissors that are dull and do not cut all the way to the point, you are doing yourself a great disservice. Dull scissors mean you will have to gnaw away at the fabric with the scissors which causes fraying and inaccuracies. The small tips are needed for getting into intricate shapes and trimming out excess fabric from behind the appliqué. I do not use the appliqué scissors with the large lip on one of the blades. They would not work for what I do. Currently, I am using the small Fiskars Softouch® micro-tip scissors that are spring-loaded. I didn't like them at first because they felt so different to use, but now that I have worked with them I think I'll be using them from now on.

THIMBLE (optional): I do not use a thimble when I appliqué. People tend to make you think you are abnormal if you don't wear a thimble, but there are lots of us non-thimble users out there...more of the politics of quilting. I do wear a hole in my middle finger after I've been appliquéing for a long time. That's when I switch from using the 12 sharps to the straw (or milliner) needle. Since the straw needle is a ½" longer than the sharps, I end up wearing a hole in a different place on my middle finger. Usually by the time that has happened the other hole has healed and I switch back to the 12 sharps. If both holes are still present in my middle finger, I put my leather thimble on to cover the sores. This forces me to use my ring finger.

62

FRAYCHECK® (optional): This product will aid you through difficult spots and its use will be detailed later.

TOOTHPICK (very optional): Some people like to use a toothpick when they do needle-turn appliqué. They claim the slight coarseness on the end of the toothpick grabs the fabric better when the seam allowances are being turned under. However, using a toothpick means you will have to set your needle down while you pick the toothpick up. This means the appliqué will take you longer to do and appliqué takes enough time already. I have no trouble getting the seam allowances to turn under with my needle, so I do not use a toothpick.

FREEZER PAPER (also very optional): I only use freezer paper when I am using a slippery fabric such as silk or polyester that I do not want to interface. To make a perfect shape such as a circle, I use freezer paper to stabilize the slippery fabric. The freezer paper is ironed to the wrong side of the fabric, and the edge of the paper then creates a stiff folding edge where the seam allowance will be turned under. The fabric does not slide around and I am able to create that perfect circle. I do not use freezer paper in any of my layering processes.

The Funky Chicken

If you have never appliquéd before or just want to hone your skills, you may want to try the Funky Chicken shape and technique sampler. You will find the pattern on the tear-out sheet.

Stitching through each step of this shape will teach you to cope with any appliqué experience. Dealing with long, straight lines, outside curves, inside curves, outside points (obtuse and acute angles), inside points, bumpy lines, and, especially, reverse appliqué are all part of making a complex appliqué picture. The Funky Chicken starts out with easy lines and then takes you through the other tricks and nuances of exacting appliqué work.

To make the Funky Chicken trace the shape onto a background cloth and then work the shape using the step-by-step instructions that follow.

Learning the Blind Stitch, Long Straight Lines, and Simple Corners

Trace the Funky Chicken onto the right side of your chosen appliqué fabric. Cut it out with a scant ¼" seam allowance. This is the usual width I cut for seam allowances. (It may be closer to ³⁄₁₆" than ¼".

Sometimes I am forced to cut narrower seam allowances, but if I have a choice, I stick with the scant ¼" cut.) Match the markings on the appliqué chicken to the markings on the background fabric and pin or baste it in place. Cut a thread no longer than 18". If you use a longer thread, it will fray and you will waste a lot of time and motion pulling the excess thread through the fabric. Thread your needle and put a quilter's knot in the end.

Quilter's Knot

Make a cross with your needle and the end of your thread under the needle. Wrap the thread around the needle two to three times clockwise looking at the point of the needle as you do when you make a French knot.

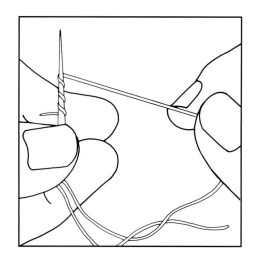

Grasping the wraps of thread between your thumb and forefinger, pull the needle through the wraps, sliding the knot down past the eye of the needle to the end of the thread. This will make the same size knot every time.

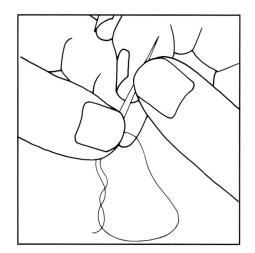

Hand Position

The way you hold your hands and arms while you are appliquéing should be natural and relaxing, with both hands resting on your lap (or a table or cushion) with the thumbs and fingers of each hand pointing toward the other. If you have to suspend one or both of your hands you could be causing undue strain to your wrists, arms, and shoulders. If, when turning the seam allowance under, you push away from yourself, you are likely to be using a stressful hand position and your results may not be successful.

Quilters need to worry about carpal tunnel syndrome. Quoting from an article by Ed Schafer of The Associated Press[2], "...unnatural postures people assume at work, home, or during sleep increase pressure on nerves or cause muscles to become too weak or too strong. Muscles work best at specific lengths. Shortened neck and shoulder muscles often become tight and painful." If you feel excess tension in your muscles while you are appliquéing, you should test other positions. I push the seam allowance toward myself which gives me good control and feels comfortable. Being right-handed, I work from right to left. If you are left-handed you will want to work from left to right. Of course, if you push the seam allowance away from yourself but you have good results and a relaxed hand position there is no reason to change.

Stitching

Using the tip of your needle, barely catch the seam allowance and fold the fabric under pushing it toward yourself at the marked seam line. The markings for the seam line should just barely disappear as you fold under the seam allowance. Hold the fold in place with your thumb. Your thumb, on top of the work, and your finger, underneath the work, act like the presser foot and feed dogs, respectively, on your sewing machine. When you are folding, there is a gap between your thumb and finger; when you are stitching, the thumb and finger are held tightly together.

Come straight up through the reverse side of your background fabric at the place marked with the asterisk on the pattern and catch two to three threads from the edge of the appliqué.

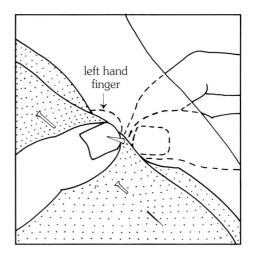

Place the tip of the needle on the fold directly across from where you came up and go straight down through the background fabric only. (This will be only one to two threads away from where you came up.) Lever the needle to come up again through the background and the fold of the appliqué a little more than $1/16$" away.

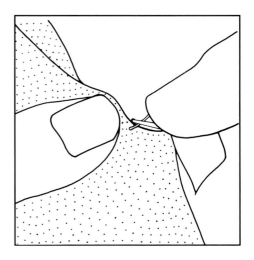

The best way I can describe the motion of the needle making an appliqué stitch is to compare it to digging a hole with a shovel. The blade of the shovel is pointed straight into the earth, and as you take that bite of earth you lever the shovel to come under that bite so you can lift it out.

[2] Ed Schafer, The Associated Press, an article in the *Salt Lake City Tribune*, Jan. 26, 1995

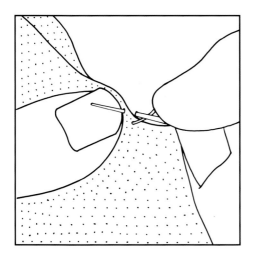

The needle is a much more delicate tool, but the technique is basically the same. It goes straight into the fabric and you take a bite (or stitch) of fabric, but you don't lift that bite of fabric out (but the point is brought up through the background), and then the fold is ready to take that next stitch. Pull the thread up until there isn't any slack remaining. The stitch should be snug, but not tight. If it is too tight your appliqué will not be smooth and may even pucker.

I average 12 to 14 stitches per inch in a line of appliqué stitches. I firmly believe this is an adequate number. I know people who possibly do 20 to 25 stitches per inch but I don't think their appliqué work looks any better than mine (and it takes them a lot more time to do). If you look at the stitches on the wrong side of your work, the stitches should have a slight slant to them.

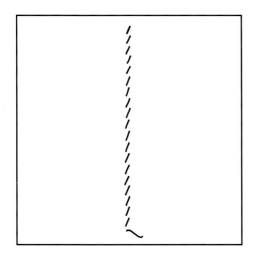

To turn the corner, stitch up to the traced point on your fabric but continue the fold line to the edge of the fabric.

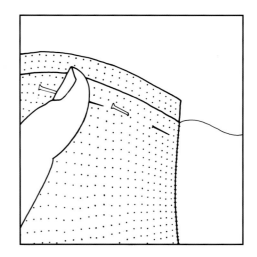

Take another stitch over the previous stitch. In other words, stitch in the same place. This will lock the corner in position. While maintaining the first fold, use the tip of your needle to fold under the other side of the corner. When the corner is shaped the way you want it, continue stitching down the other side.

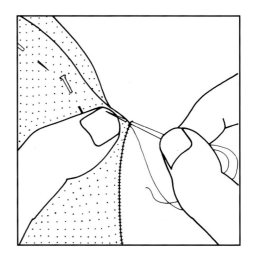

You will probably still have thread left in your needle at this point, and possibly enough to stitch several more inches. If you are ready to tie off, however, you should pass the needle through the background to the reverse side of the work as if you were going down for the first part of the appliqué stitch. As you are picking up a few threads of background fabric, make a loop, pass the needle through it, make another loop, and then pass the needle through again. In other words, just make a simple knot. Cut your thread leaving a ¼" tail.

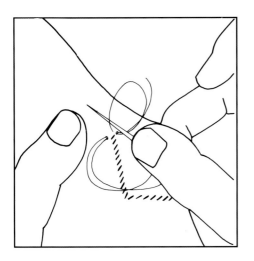

A primary rule for doing good appliqué is to not stitch it down until it looks the way you want it. Keep your focus small. The only shaping of the appliqué to worry about is the next four or five (or less) stitches you'll work, or whatever is under your thumb. Don't be concerned with anything further past the location of your needle, thread, and thumb.

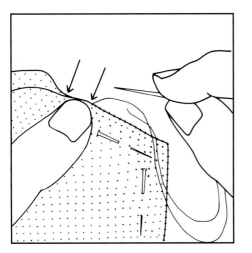

Stitching an Outside Curve

Many appliqué instructions will tell you to clip or notch (V) an outside (convex) curve. This is totally unnecessary. The fullness created in the seam allowance of an outside curve is gradually eased in as you progress around the curve. (Using the tip that tells you to only worry about what's under your thumb comes in handy here.) Catch the seam allowance with the tip of your needle and push it under a bit at a time. Sometimes the fold may have a slight bump or corner which disturbs the smoothness of the curve. It usually means the seam allowance has formed a tuck while it was being turned under. Don't stitch it down until it is correct. As you are working underneath the appliqué, use the point of your needle to pull the seam allowance to the left or right to work the tuck out.

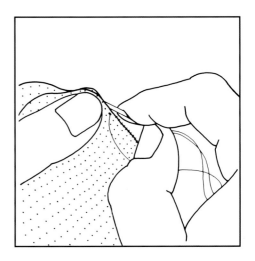

Stitching an Inside Curve

Clipping an inside (concave) curve is necessary or the seam allowance will not turn under properly. Clips should be made to the line, but not across the line (remember that those lines do have width) and be made often enough that the seam allowance will turn under easily without forming minor indentations. An inside curve should be as smooth as an outside curve. When clipping the seam allowance of the sampler section with the gradual inside curves, clips should be made every ³⁄₈" to ¹⁄₂".

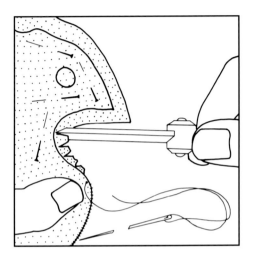

On the tight inside curves, you will need to clip every ¹⁄₄" and even closer. Catch the seam allowance with the tip of your needle, but away from where you have clipped. Use the side of your needle to push the seam allowance under to where the fold starts to form a dimple at the base of the next clip. This ensures that the raw edges of the clip are well underneath the appliqué. Pushing with the side of your needle involves a sweeping, counterclockwise movement (clockwise if you are left-handed) with your needle and wrist.

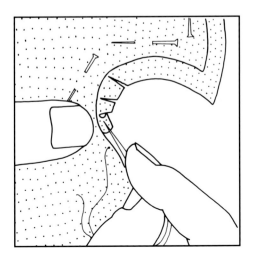

Stitching an Outside Point

Fold the seam allowance of the first side of the point so the fold continues past the point to the edge of the fabric. Stitch to where the point is marked on the fabric. Take an extra stitch on top of your last one to lock the point in place. Now peel back the appliqué to expose the seam allowance you have just stitched down.

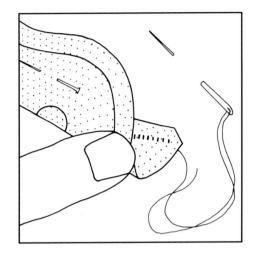

Since this seam has already been stitched down, you don't need this much seam allowance anymore. Trim the seam allowance close to the stitching (to about ¹⁄₁₆") under the point.

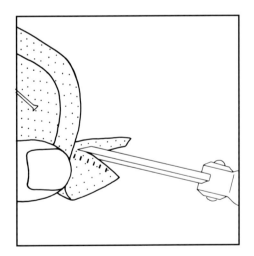

Lay the appliqué back down and trim the seam allowance at the point to about ⅛", also trimming the other side of the point to about ⅛".

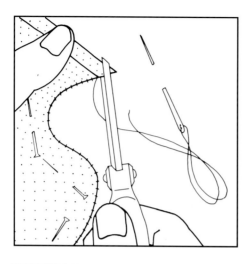

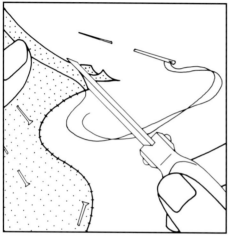

Your appliqué should look like the illustration.

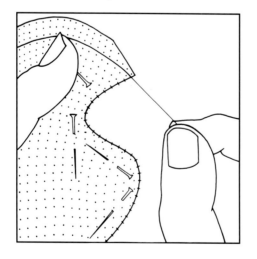

Using the tip of the needle to turn this narrow seam allowance under, make a perpendicular fold.

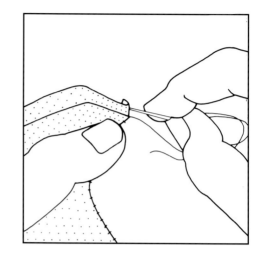

Put your thumb on top of this fold and press it in place. Now use the tip of the needle inserted in that fold to make a second fold along the seam line of the other side of the point.

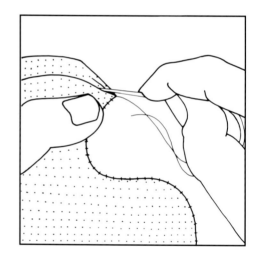

You may have to push on this fold more than once to work it under. Before resuming stitching, give the thread (which is coming from the last stitch at the point) a tug. This will straighten out the tip of the appliqué and make it as "pointy" as possible. If there seems to be too much bulk from the seam allowance hanging out and making an obstacle to stitch around, come up through the background at a point you think the fold should be lying on. Bring the tip of needle around the bulk that is hanging out and then through the folded seam line of your appliqué. Pull the thread tight. This should force any unwanted bulk under the appliqué.

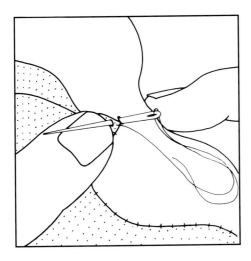

Continue stitching down the side of the point. When you get to the head of the chicken the curves become bumpy and then very sharp. The seam allowance cannot help but have tucks in it around this part of the shape. The trick is to disperse those tucks evenly and flatten the bumps out by smashing them down a bit with the side of the needle before stitching them down. A tight outside curve should still look relatively smooth. These involved shapes must be mastered for you to be able to portray figures and other nuances of form. You need to be able to coax these subtleties out of the fabric.

Subtle Curves: One or two clips will be needed in the inside curves. Fold the entire seam allowance under from one inside curve to the next. Then using the tip of your needle to manipulate the seam line and using light pressure from your thumb, pull the fabric up to form the outside curve. Hold tight with your thumb while stitching in place.

Sharp Curves: Now the seam line makes a sharp U-turn. You will need to slow down here just as you would slow down considerably for a U-turn if you were driving. You may want to trim the seam allowance to ⅛" around this curve. Make tiny tucks as you move around the curve and only worry about what the shape looks like for the next two or three stitches ahead.

Stitching an Inside Point (Deep Clip)

Clip straight into the deepest part of the inside corner, dividing the seam allowances as evenly as possible with the clip. Again, clip to the line but not across the line.

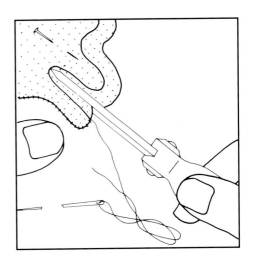

Work with the seam allowance on one side of the clip at a time. Tuck under the seam allowance on the right side of the clip, pushing until the fold at the base of the clip starts to dimple.

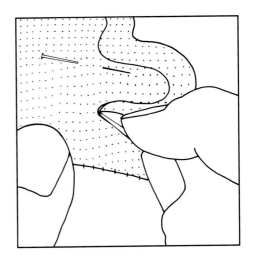

Stitch down to the base of the clip. At the base of the clip, come up through the background and the appliqué three to four threads below the last cut thread. Make another stitch right on top of the clip and pull it tight. This secures the clip.

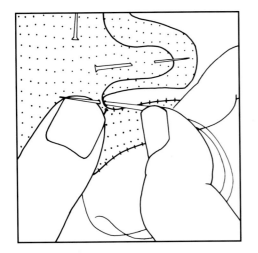

Now work the other side of the clip. Catch the seam allowance with your needle well above the clip.

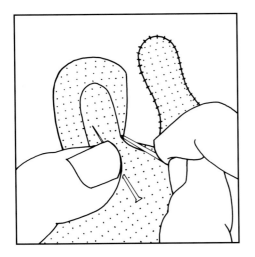

(Never dig at the clip with your needle or it will fray.) Using the side of the needle, roll the seam allowance underneath by moving the needle until it comes to rest at the base of the clip and twisting it gradually counterclockwise (clockwise for lefties). This should tuck under any seam allowance and any straying threads. If any small bits of thread are still poking out at the base of the clip, try the twisting motion again with the side of the needle or use the tip of the needle to push them under the fold. Continue stitching the other side.

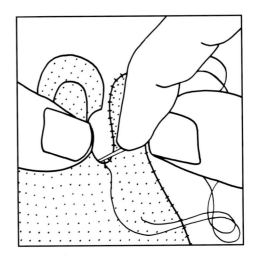

Inside points or very deep inside curves or narrow channels are places where you may want to consider using Fraycheck®. This product is, as the name suggests, a fraying preventative. You can use it to make your appliqué a less stressful experience by adding it in places where your fabric may have frayed.

Fraycheck will stain or change the color of your fabric; don't apply it anywhere where it will be seen. Use it only for seam allowances (where the fabric will be turned under and the treated fabric will be out of sight). If you were to just squirt it out of the bottle onto your fabric, you would have no control over how much comes out and you would probably end up getting it places that you don't want it. To remedy this situation, I "paint" the Fraycheck onto my seam allowances. I squeeze a small bead of it out at the applicator end of the bottle, and then, using a pin or a toothpick, I take that bead of Fraycheck and paint it into narrow seam allowances such as the deep clip of an inside point or curve or a narrow channel between the marked seam lines.

"painting" with Fraycheck

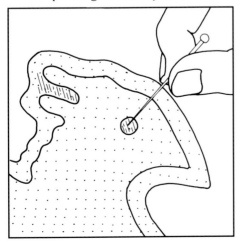

Let the Fraycheck dry for five to ten minutes. Once dry, go ahead and appliqué as normal, but the seam allowance should fold under easily where the Fraycheck ends without any fraying—if you have done your "painting" accurately. If you happen to make a mistake with the Fraycheck, all is not lost. The liquid is removable when wet. Use rubbing alcohol on a cotton swab to remove it from your fabric (careful of color changes, though). Once it has dried it cannot be removed. However, Fraycheck is such a wonderful aid that I do not get overly concerned about what it might do to fabrics in the long run. It has not caused any damage, that I can see, to some of the pieces I made six or more years ago.

While working the series of bumpy curves you will need to follow all the directions for making inside curves and outside curves but they will be concentrated and repeated one after the other.

Zig-zags: This can be the hardest appliqué to do. Each line before it turns a corner is only three or four stitches long. Some people tend to get stressed out over this and overwork the fabric which causes fraying. Follow the directions for inside and outside points. You will have to clip the next inside point before working on the outside point. Practice is needed to make these points precise.

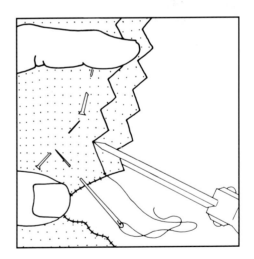

Reverse Appliqué

Judy Mathieson told me of an analogy she heard about appliqué. Imagine yourself as a cliff diver on a small island in the middle of the ocean with only the cliffs for a shoreline. The top of the island is your piece of appliqué and the ocean is your background fabric. You dive straight down into the ocean (taking a downward stitch) off the edge of a cliff. Clambering out of the water and scaling the cliff slantwise (bringing your needle under the background fabric) you arrive on top of the island (coming up through the fold of the appliqué) only to dive into the ocean again and repeat the whole process. I think the story bears an apt resemblance to the appliqué process. Well, if diving off an island into the ocean is the way to think of appliqué, think of diving into a lake or, even better, a water-filled quarry, as an analogy for reverse appliqué. The land around the water is what you are appliquéing down and the water is your underneath layer or background. The techniques for diving and scaling the cliffs (stitching) are the same. The shapes are just layered differently. Some people seem to be intimidated by the words reverse appliqué, but you are doing essentially the same thing when you do plain appliqué and, for some shapes, it is much easier to use reverse appliqué.

The eye and the wing of the Funky Chicken are reverse appliquéed. Start with the eye and clip it out to form a star or asterisk in the top layer of fabric. (You may want to add Fraycheck to this tiny circle before working on it.)

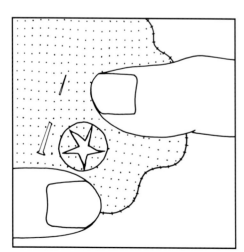

Use the side of your needle and a twisting motion with your wrist to tuck the seam allowance under and stitch the edges down. This tiny shape is much easier to do in reverse appliqué than it would be to do in regular appliqué.

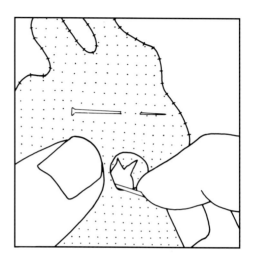

The wing is two-colored and is designed to give you a bit of experience in my layering technique. Separate the two layers. Using your fine-tipped scissors, nip a hole in the top fabric. Cut a seam allowance (all cutting is being done inside the reverse appliqué shape) which should reveal the fabric underneath. Now, using all the techniques you used to make the outside of the sampler shape, stitch the reverse appliqué shape. Start at the designated point and work only the upper portions of the seam line where the white part of the wing joins the body of the chicken.

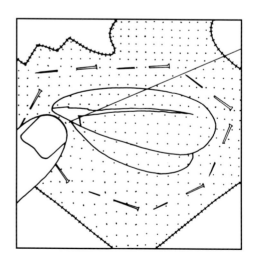

Baste across the lower portion of the white area of the wing to hold the two fabrics together.

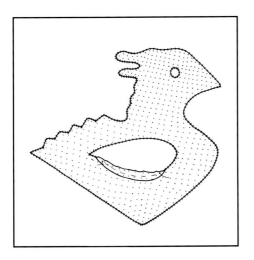

Once the outside edge of the chicken and the reverse appliqué seam lines that connect to the background have been sewn, the excess background fabric behind the shape needs to be trimmed away. Separate the two layers of fabric and snip an opening with your fine-tipped scissors. Then trim away the excess background fabric to a scant ¼", being careful not to cut the top layer. The wrong side of the work should look like the illustration (below).

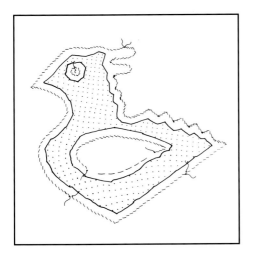

Turn back to the right side and redraw the missing seam line for the bottom portion of the white wing onto the background fabric.

Pin a piece of contrasting fabric behind the lower portion of the wing.

No markings need to be made on this fabric.

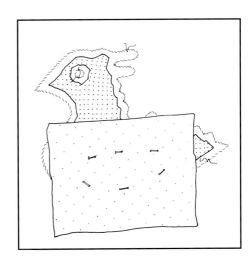

Remove the basting and, clipping where necessary, push back the seam allowances to reveal the contrasting fabric. Stitch the lower wing fabric in place.

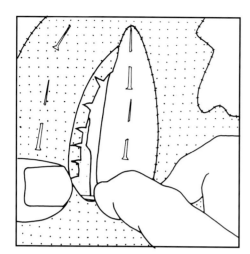

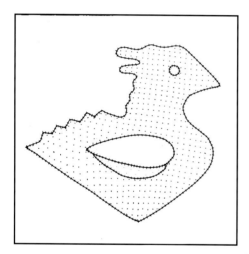

After stitching, the wrong side of the work will look like the illustration.

Trim away the excess leaving a scant ¼" seam allowance; the project is now finished.

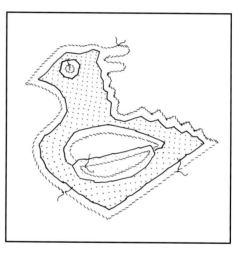

That's all there is to it. The stitching is the same, just the layering is different. No need to work up a sweat when someone mentions reverse appliqué.

Once you have honed you appliqué skills, you are ready to go on to the projects in the next chapter.

MADE IN AMERICA, 1992, 70" x 80", Alex Anderson.
(Photo: M. K. Mahoney, courtesy *Quilter's Newsletter Magazine*)
Alex began making the eagle for this quilt in one of my classes,
using a piece of clip art for reference. The title stems from the
controversy surrounding cheap, imported quilts being sold in
the United States.

FOUR SEASONS, 1993, 47½" x 47", Kathy Jevne Clark. (Photo: D. Larsen) This quilt shows how an apple tree's branches go through a year of changes.

"He who works with his hands is a laborer; He who works with his hand and his head is an artisan; He who works with his hand and his head and his heart is an artist."

T.V. Smith

BIRDS A-HUMMING, IRIS A-BLOOMING, 1990, 60" x 80", Joan Rollins. (Photo: DSI Studios, courtesy American Quilter's Society) A traditional quilt with pictorial aspects, the opalescent lamé used in the quilt makes the throats of the hummingbirds shimmer.

CHAPTER SEVEN

STITCH BY NUMBER

Layering Up or Down?

I have given my best advice for picking a subject, using photos and projecting them, drawing a pattern, choosing fabrics and appliquéing them. It is now time to apply this advice to make pictorial appliqué quilts.

First you'll need to determine which layering process is best to use. According to most definitions of appliqué (with some exceptions), when you layer from the back (as with Baltimore blocks), you are appliquéing; when you layer from the top down (as with a mola), you are reverse appliquéing. I have a little bit of a problem with this definition because I do not think it is this cut-and-dried. But it will serve for now.

Up or down...which way to work? I start by examining what needs to be done for each section and then decide on the appropriate method. If I am making figures (people, animals, sometimes buildings) I most often layer from the top layer down. These figures end up being independent of the rest of the quilt. I can then arrange them on a background that is suitable. However, a landscape (which might even be the background for a figure) needs to be layered from the object furthest from you (as it would exist in reality) to the thing closest to you, so I layer from the back layer to the top layer.

As I've already stated, the little I knew of appliqué came from watching my friend Jeana work on one of her pieces and working together with my quilting group on an appliqué quilt—a wall hanging of a Victorian house. I learned many lessons from that small project, the main one being that I did not like the buildup of layers when working up from the back layer. The layers were miserable to quilt through. And even if they were trimmed away, the layers still had little bridges of fabric remaining along the seam lines that got in the way. But building up from the back layer is how most appliqué is worked.

When I decided I had to make a Liberty quilt for the first Great American Quilt Contest, I knew the only way to get a realistic portrayal of the Statue of Liberty was with appliqué. Having had only the experience of that small wall hanging, I had to come up with my own techniques to make the shaded and dimensional-looking appliqué. After thinking through how everything should come together, I decided it would be easiest to layer my fabrics if I worked from the top layer down. Basing my decision on my little appliqué experience, I didn't know that most people don't work this way. However, the process I go through to make these shaded figures is a very logical and well thought-out method. It just seems foreign to quilters with a traditional appliqué background.

In my class description for the "Appliqué for Realism" workshop, I recommend the class for the advanced student. While it is a difficult and tricky technique, I find that it is not always the experienced quilter who is the most successful at first. While teaching a six hour class in an eastern state, I had as a student a woman who was a very experienced quilter—she had just been featured in an article for a national quilting magazine. This woman was somewhat confounded by my technique, not because she lacked the skills—her skills were obviously tremendous—but because she seemed unable to get past her predisposition about how appliqué should be done. In the same class, I had a student who was exactly the opposite. He arrived two hours late, so he missed all the preliminary explanations. (Six hour classes in this subject are difficult to teach because the students only get a very hasty sampling of the layering techniques. I prefer doing two or more day classes.) He was Swiss and spoke only a little English. And he had never appliquéed before. After filling him in as much as I could without neglecting the rest of the class, I sent him off to work. He caught right on to the layering process and though his appliqué techniques and stitches were quite terrible, when he left the workshop he had a face emerging in his class project.

The moral of this story: try to tuck all those preconceived notions away about how an appliqué figure is put together so they won't get tangled up with what I'm telling you in this chapter.

The projects in this book are designed to help you understand how these layering techniques work. Hopefully, after working one or more of the projects you will catch on to the processes and realize what a logical way of working it is. Making one or all of the projects will give you the experience you need to create pictorial quilts drawn from your own imagination and/or photos.

This chapter contains three projects for pictorial figures. The next chapter will detail making a landscape project. When making figures and faces I always layer from the top down—though every once in a while a small piece may be layered on top. The projects range in difficulty. The Dancer's Head is the easiest, Anthony (the rabbit) is slightly more difficult, and Samantha is the hardest. I recommend you start with the Dancer's Head; it will give you the clearest sense of the how the layering sequence works.

"The object of art is
to give life a shape."

Jean Anouilh
[The Rehearsal, Act I, sc. ii]

THE DANCER'S HEAD

I advise you to use shades of gray fabric to create this project. You can try it in flesh tones but these colors are harder to find and it is more difficult to make them look right. You will need four shades for her face, two shades (one can be black) of dark tones for her hair, and two lighter shades for her hair ribbon. I like making her hair and the ribbon from different hues of gray, such as blue-gray or brown-gray, to give the impression of separate entities.

You will need to trace the pattern from the tear-out at the back of the book on to another piece of white paper. This is so you can use the pattern on a light box without being confused by the pattern lines for the projects printed on the other side of the sheet.

FACE 1

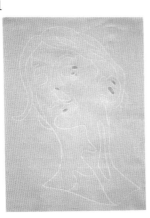

Cut a piece of your lightest gray face fabric (Number 1) ½" larger than the entire pattern (about 9" x 12"). Place your pattern on the light box and put the fabric over the top of it. Trace the whole Dancer's Head on to the fabric using a removable marker.

(Fabric is wasted by cutting this much, but working this way helps prevent mistakes caused by cutting too little fabric. When you've gotten familiar with the process, you will know how much fabric you should cut. Trust me.) At this point, if you feel some of these shapes are too small for you to handle easily and that you may have fraying, you can use Fraycheck®. As described in Chapter Six, paint only in the small corners and channels that will be worked in the Number 1 fabric. This step is optional.

FACE 2

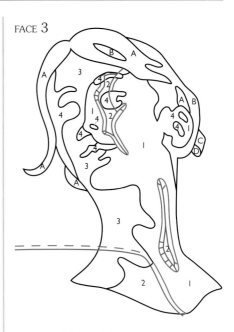

Place your next lightest shade of face fabric (Number 2) behind the Number 1 fabric. No markings are made on this fabric at this time. Pin (or baste) the two fabrics together around the shapes where Number 1 seam lines join Number 2 seam lines placing pins in the Number 1 fabric.

FACE 3

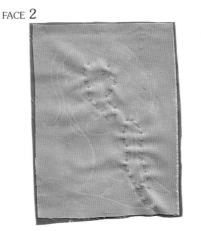

At this point you may cut anywhere in the top layer of fabric that is not labeled Number 1. Seam allowances are cut around the Number 1 shapes revealing Number 2 fabric as shown by the green lines in the illustration.

Do not clip into any corners unnecessarily—they may not be actual corners. For example, any lines connecting with the outside edges of the figure are not actual corners—the cutting lines extend out past the edge and are part of the seam allowance when the finished figure is appliquéd to a background. The red lines in the illustration represent the actual seam lines to be stitched.

FACE 4

When stitching is complete your work should look like the photo. Be sure to baste across her neck and eyebrow as shown. The basting thread holds the layers together and helps maintain the flatness of the work. It also helps aid in trimming away of the excess fabric from the back of the work.

FACE 5

Now return to the light box and realign your work on top of the pattern. On fabric Number 2 redraw any missing pattern lines. By marking the Number 2 fabric after it is sewn in place you don't have to bother with matching seam lines. This also assures the integrity and accuracy of the figure.

FACE 6

You have two layers of fabric at this point. If you don't get rid of the excess now you will have a buildup of layers. Excess fabric will get in the way of the following layers. Carefully trim the excess Number 2 fabric away to a scant ¼" seam allowance as shown in the photograph.

FACE 7

Now place face fabric Number 3 behind the work. Place pins inside the Number 1 and 2 fabrics everywhere a seam line joins the Number 3 fabric.

FACE 8

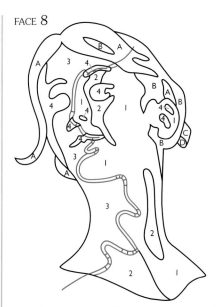

Cut a seam allowance around the Number 1 and 2 shapes. Do not cut the Number 3 fabric.

FACE 9

The seam line that is worked on this layer essentially divides the face down the middle and you'll need to cut the two lighter layers away from the right side of the face. When the stitching is complete it should look like the photograph.

Return the work to the light box, realign on pattern and redraw any missing lines on fabric Number 3.

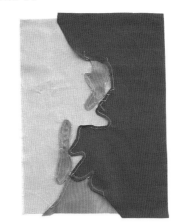

You may want to apply Fraycheck® to the smaller areas of Number 3 that are to be worked next. Turn back to the wrong side and then trim away the excess Number 3 fabric from under the lighter fabrics.

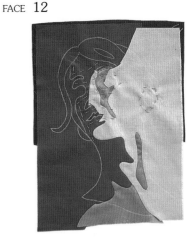

Face fabric Number 4 (the darkest) is placed behind the work. This piece need only be cut big enough to adequately cover all the Number 4 shapes. Place pins in the Number 1, 2, and 3 fabrics around the Number 4 shapes. This layer will seem most like the type of reverse appliqué you are use to doing.

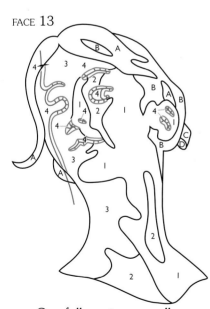

Carefully cut seam allowances (green lines in the illustration) in the Number 4 shapes.

Push the seam allowances back to reveal the Number 4 fabric. Do not cut the Number 4 fabric. Complete the stitching as shown in the photograph.

Return to the light box, realign the work with the pattern and redraw any missing lines on fabric Number 4.

FACE 16

Trim away the excess Number 4 fabric so the wrong side looks like the photograph. The face portion of the head is now complete. It should be one layer of fabric except at the seam allowances—just like a pieced block except that you have worked in appliqué.

HAIR 1

Now take the darker of the fabrics you have selected for the hair (Fabric A) and trace the entire hair onto it plus a ½" or so of any of the face lines that intersect the hair (for matching purposes).

HAIR 2

Place the lighter of the hair fabrics (Fabric B) under it and pin in Fabric A along the seam lines joining Fabric B.

HAIR 3

Cut, stitch, and baste as shown in the photograph.

HAIR 4

Return to the light box, realign and redraw any missing lines on Fabric B.

HAIR 5

Trim to look like the photograph. The hair is now complete.

HAIR 6

Trim the hairline of the face down to a seam allowance and, matching the marked lines, pin the face on top of the hair. (Doing the opposite—trimming the hair down to a seam allowance and placing it on top of the face—would also work, but I think the first method is easier.) Stitch in place, changing thread colors to match as you go.

HEAD 1

Make the ribbon as you did the hair: trace onto Fabric C, pin on top of Fabric D, stitch to joining seam line, and then redraw missing line on Fabric D. Trim down to the seam allowance except where it goes under the hair, and then pin under hair and stitch in place.

HEAD 2

The wrong side of the work should look like the photograph.

HEAD 3

Trim away excess from the ends of the ribbon and the hair fabrics from under the face as shown in the photograph.

HEAD 4

The Dancer's Head is now complete. What you have just constructed is essentially a cut out similar to what you would buy off the bolt at the fabric store.

You know, those cute little bunnies and teddy bears and ducks that you're supposed to cut out of the fabric with a seam allowance and appliqué onto a pillow or quilt.

Only you've done all the work of making the cut-out. Now you can appliqué it anywhere you please: a pillow, wall hanging, back of a jacket.

Pin the Dancer's Head to your selected background. Matching thread to fabric as you work around the outside of the head, stitch the figure to the background.

If you are making a quilt or a wall hanging, you will want to cut the excess background fabric from behind the Dancer's Head to eliminate the extra layer. Doing this will make quilting easier and make the appliqué lie smooth and flat without any puckers. The appliqué for this project is now complete.

ANTHONY
THE RABBIT

To make Anthony you need four shades of white to medium gray fabric for his fur or body, two shades of pink for his eye, ears, and nose, two shades of blue for his eye, and a scrap of light gray for the white of his eye. I used the back side of a mottled gray and white fabric for Number 1, the back side of a mottled gray fabric for Number 2, the right side of the Number 2 fabric for Number 3, and a mottled darker gray for Number 4. I chose these fabrics to simulate the texture of fur. The pink and blue fabrics also had some mottling in them. The fabrics chosen for the background were selected for their resemblance to straw in a hutch or barn.

You will need to trace the pattern from the tear-out at the back of the book onto another piece of white paper. This is so you can use the pattern on a light box without being confused by the pattern lines for the projects on the other side of the sheet.

"God is really only another artist. He invented the giraffe, the elephant and the cat. He has no real style, He just goes on trying other things. "

Pablo Picasso

EAR 1

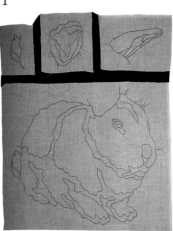

Trace the entire figure onto the Number 1 fabric.

Put the pattern on the light box with fabric Number 1 on top of it. Trace with a removable marker. Notice how the ears and tail are traced on separate rectangles of fabric. Anthony has places where Number 1 shapes meet Number 1 shapes and Number 2 shapes meet Number 2 shapes. These sections need to be worked separately to achieve a seam line between shapes of the same color.

EAR 2

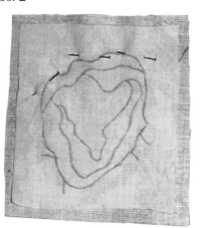

Start with his right ear first. Pin a piece of fabric Number 2 behind Number 1.

No markings are made on Number 2 yet.

EAR 3

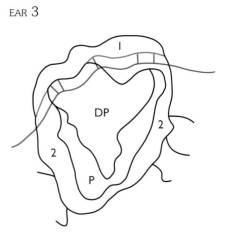

Cut a seam allowance (as shown by the green lines in the illustration) for the lower edge of the shape labeled Number 1 and stitch only where shape Number 1 joins shape Number 2 (the red lines). Do not cut fabric Number 2.

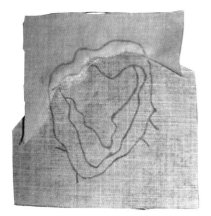

Baste across the seam allowance remaining in between the two lines of stitching. Return to the light box, realign the fabric to the pattern and redraw any missing lines.

Turn the work to the wrong side and trim away excess Number 2 fabric.

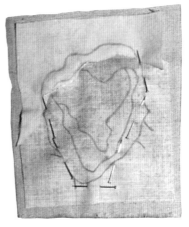

Place a piece of the lighter pink fabric behind the work. Pin in the Number 2 fabric along where the seam line adjoins the pink.

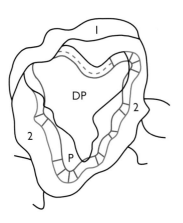

Cut as shown by green lines in the illustration and stitch along the red lines. Do not cut the pink fabric. Baste across fabric Number 2.

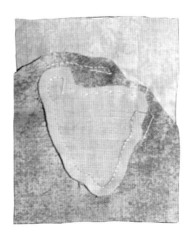

Turn the work to the wrong side and trim away the excess fabric as shown.

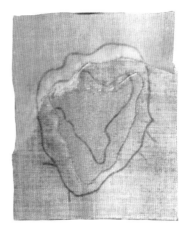

Return to the light box, realign the pattern and the fabric, and redraw any missing lines on the pink fabric.

EAR 10

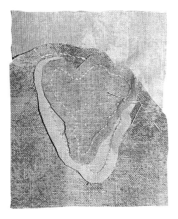

Place a piece of the darker pink fabric behind the work. Pin in Number 1 and 2 and the pink fabric around the shape labeled dark pink. Remove basting.

EAR 11

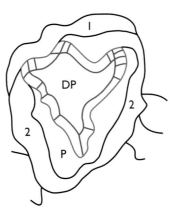

Cut as shown by green lines in the illustration and stitch along the red lines, changing thread to match the fabric. Do not cut the dark pink fabric. Stitching should meet where you started on this layer.

EAR 12

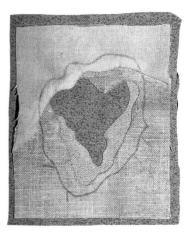

The ear should look like the photo when stitching is completed.

EAR 13

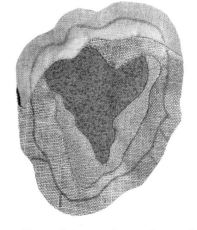

Turn the work to the wrong side and trim away the excess fabric.

EAR 14

Trim the ear from the right side to seam allowances all the way around. The right ear is now complete.

BODY 1

The next step is to work Anthony's body. Place a piece of fabric Number 2 behind the Number 1 fabric with the lines traced on it. No markings are made on fabric Number 2. Pin inside shapes of Number 1 that adjoin Number 2 shapes.

BODY 2

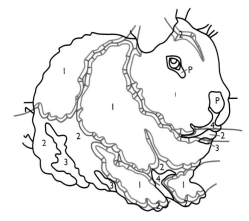

Cut down the narrow channels revealing fabric Number 2. Cut as shown by green lines in the illustration and stitch along the red lines. Do not cut fabric Number 2.

BODY 3

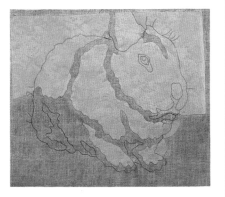

Baste where indicated and when stitching is done the work should look similar to that shown in the photo.

Return to the light box, realign the pattern and the fabric, and redraw any missing lines on Number 2.

BODY 4

Turn the work to the wrong side and trim away the excess fabric. The wrong side should look like the photo.

BODY 5

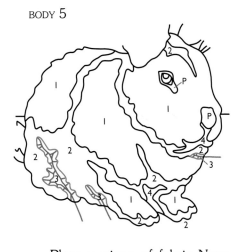

Place a piece of fabric Number 3 behind, making sure it is large enough to cover all the shapes labeled Number 3. Pin in Number 1 and 2 around the Number 3 shapes. Cut as shown by green lines in the illustration and stitch along the red lines. Do not cut fabric Number 3.

BODY 6

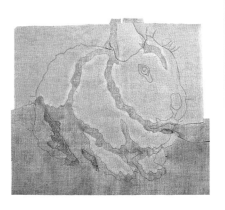

Remove basting where necessary during this step. When this step is completed it should look like the photo.

Return to the light box, realign the pattern and the fabric, and redraw any missing lines on Number 3 (there won't be very many).

BODY 7

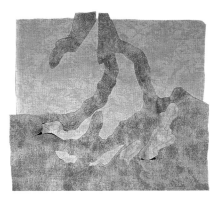

Turn the work to the wrong side and trim away the excess fabric.

(Note that Number 3 areas on the wrong side of the project look lighter in color than Number 2 areas because the back side of this fabric was used for the front side of Number 2.)

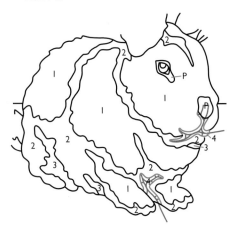

Place small pieces of Number 4 fabric (enough to cover the Number 4 shapes) behind the work. Pin in Number 1 and 2 around the Number 4 shapes. Cut as shown by green lines in the illustration and stitch along the red lines. Do not cut fabric Number 4.

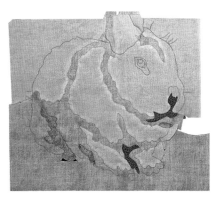

Project will look like the photo. Trim away the excess Number 4 fabric from the wrong side, re-align the pattern and fabric on the light box, and re-draw any missing lines (just some short ones on the outside edges).

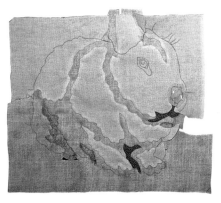

Trace the nose onto the lighter pink fabric, cut out with a seam allowance, and pin in place on top, matching the lines. Stitch in place.

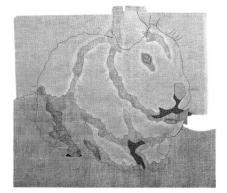

Reverse appliqué the pink shape around the eye by pinning a piece of the lighter pink fabric behind the eye. (You may want to Fraycheck® the corners of the eye beforehand.) When stitching is completed, realign the project with the pattern on the light box and redraw the eye details. Trim away excess pink fabric from wrong side.

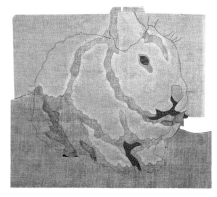

Pin the lighter blue fabric behind the eye shape. If you want to do a simple eye, ignore the iris, pupil, and eye white, and reverse appliqué around the entire eye oval. Trim away the excess blue fabric from the wrong side and the simple eye is complete.

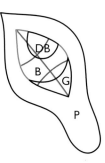

If you want to make the detailed eye, cut on green lines and stitch on the red lines (only where blue joins pink).

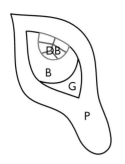

Redraw the shape of the iris and pupil on the blue fabric. Trim away the excess blue fabric to ⅛" seam allowances. Pin a small piece of the darker blue fabric behind the eye. Cut on green lines, carefully clipping out the tiny pupil hole and stitch on the red lines.

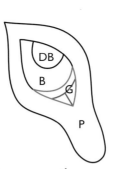

Trim away the excess dark blue fabric from the wrong side. Pin a small piece of light gray fabric behind the eye to make the eye white. Most of the cutting is already done but cuts are made on the green lines and stitch on the red lines. Trim away the excess light gray fabric from the wrong side. The detailed eye is now complete.

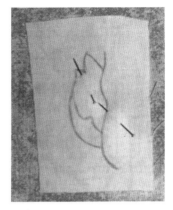

To make the tail pin a piece of Number 2 fabric behind the Number 1 fabric with the tail marked on it.

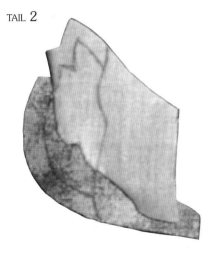

Cut a seam allowance and stitch seam line where Number 1 adjoins Number 3. Trim around tail leaving a seam allowance but leave a large allowance to pin tail under his body.

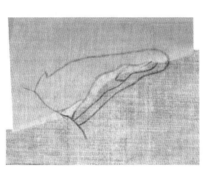

To make the left ear pin a piece of fabric Number 2 behind the marked Number 1. Stitch Number 1 fabric down to Number 2 fabric only where they adjoin. Baste the remaining seam allowance.

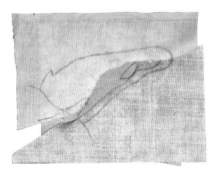

Redraw any missing lines. Trim away excess Number 2 from wrong side. Pin a piece of the lighter pink behind the work. Remove basting, trim seam allowances on Number 1 and 2 fabrics and stitch in place. Redraw any missing lines.

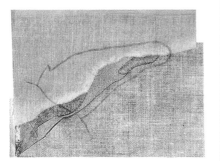

Trim away the excess pink fabric from the wrong side. Pin a piece of Number 3 fabric behind the ear. Stitch in small areas of Number 3.

Redraw any missing lines. Trim seam allowance around ear except where it goes under the head. Trim any excess Number 3 fabric from wrong side of work. The left ear is now complete.

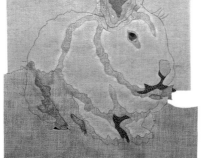

Pin Anthony's right ear on top of his head matching the marked lines. Stitch in place only where ear connects to head (not around outside edges).

Trim away excess body fabrics from under ear. Cut remaining outside edges of body down to a seam allowance.

FIGURE 1

Pin Anthony's tail and left ear under his body and head matching marked lines.

Stitch in place only where tail and ear connect to body and head (no outside edges). Trim away excess tail and ear fabric from under body. Anthony's body is now complete.

FIGURE 2

You have made another cut-out to appliqué where you want. Compose your background and then pin him in place.

FIGURE 3

Stitch around all the outside edges matching the thread to the fabric as you go. Cut out the excess background fabric from behind the figure. You now have a finished appliqué of Anthony.

SAMANTHA

Sam has lovely light-chocolate colored skin, so you will need to find five suitable brown fabrics for her. The first time I made her I used the Color Bars® fabric (seven solid shades printed onto one fabric) but wasn't truly pleased with the results. I did her again using fabrics from different manufacturers. For her face you will need four browns ranging from medium to dark and then another one that is the darkest brown you can find (you can get away with four browns because the darkest fifth color is used for her left eyebrow only); two shades of red for her lips (I did use the red Color Bars fabric for them); three shades of light to medium gray for the whites of her eyes; and black for her pupils. For her hair you will need black and another differently hued brown and for her clothing you will need two shades of burgundy, along with a muted print background of your choice.

You will need to trace the pattern from the tear-out at the back of the book on to another piece of white paper. This is so you can use the pattern on a light box without being confused by the pattern lines for the projects on the other side of the tear-out.

FACE 1

Start her face by cutting a rectangle large enough to cover her whole face (with 1" extra around the outside) from the lightest of the skin colors (Number 1). Place the pattern on the light box with the fabric over the top and draw all of the face along with about a ½" of any lines from the hair or neck that intersect the face.

FACE 2

Cut a piece of skin fabric Number 2 the same size as the Number 1. No markings are made on this fabric yet. Place the Number 2 fabric behind Number 1 and pin the Number 1 shapes in place where they join the Number 2 shapes.

FACE 3

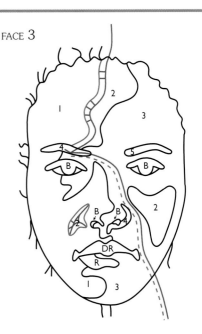

Remember that you can cut anywhere in the Number 1 fabric that is not labeled as a Number 1 shape. Cut on the green lines as shown in illustration and stitch on the red lines. Do not cut the Number 2 fabric.

There are only two places to actually appliqué on this layer: the line coming down across her forehead and the dimple on the right side of her face.

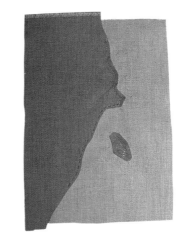

A line of basting stitches is necessary so you can cut away the Number 1 layer from the left side of the face to reveal the Number 2 layer. Return to the light box, re-align the pattern and the fabric and redraw any lines that are missing on the Number 2 fabric.

Turn to the wrong side of the work and trim away the excess Number 2 fabric from behind the Number 1 fabric to a seam allowance.

At this point you may want to paint Fraycheck® into the tiny corners and channels as shown.

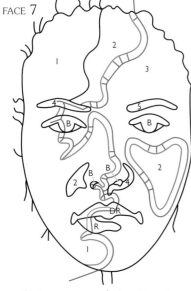

Cut a piece of the Number 3 skin fabric the same size as the first two and place it behind the work. Pin in the Number 1 and 2 shapes where they join the Number 3 shapes. Cut on the green lines as shown in the illustration and stitch on the red lines. Do not cut the Number 3 fabric.

The photograph shows the cut seam allowance at this stage.

The photograph shows completed stitching for this layer.

Return the work to the light box, realign the pattern and the fabric and redraw any lines that are missing on the Number 3 fabric.

Trim away the excess Number 3 fabric from under the previous layers so the wrong side looks like the photograph. You may want to apply Fraycheck® in the tiny corners of fabric Number 3 at this point.

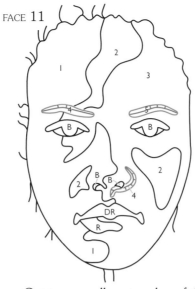

Cut two small rectangles of the Number 4 skin fabric that will be big enough to cover the Number 4 shapes and one of Number 5 for the left eyebrow. (You can make these all the same fabric if you couldn't find a fifth fabric). Pin these fabrics behind the work in the appropriate places. Cut on the green lines as shown in the illustration and stitch on the red lines.

The resulting work should look like the photograph. Redraw the lines for the nostrils that are missing. Trim the excess Number 4 and 5 fabrics to a seam allowance around the eyebrows and nose.

Cut a rectangle of black fabric big enough to fit behind both of the eyes and the nostrils. Pin the fabric in place behind the work. Cut on the green lines as shown in the illustration and stitch only on the red lines.

Knot off each time you stop, matching thread to the fabric as you stitch. The resulting work should look like the photograph.

Return the work to the light box, realign the pattern and the fabric and redraw any lines that are missing on the black fabric. Trim away excess fabric to a narrow seam allowance around the eyes and nostrils.

EYE 1

EYE 2

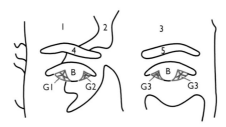

EYE 3

I used three different gray fabrics to make Sam's eye whites, working each shade one at a time. Place a small square of the lightest gray behind the outside corner of her right eye. Cut on the green lines as shown in the illustration and stitch only on the red lines. Reverse appliqué the small triangle and trim away the excess gray fabric. Place

a small square of the next lightest gray behind the inside corner of her right eye. Stitch and then trim away any excess. Place a small rectangle of the darker gray fabric behind her left eye. Stitch both sides of the eye white and trim away excess. The first photograph shows the wrong side of the work with eye whites in progress.

The photograph shows right side with whites completed.

LIPS 1

STEP ONE

STEP TWO

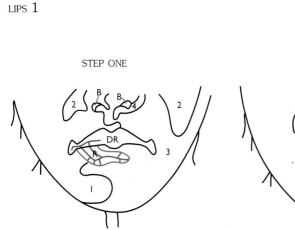
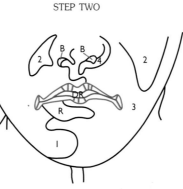

LIPS 2

Work the lips separately. Work the lower lip first by cutting a piece of the lighter red fabric and pinning it in place behind the work. Cut on the green lines as shown in illustration (step one) and stitch on the red lines.

Trim away excess fabric from behind. Cut a piece of the darker red fabric for her upper lip and pin in place behind the work. Cut on the green lines as shown in step two of the illustration and stitch on the red lines.

The completed face should look like the photograph.

LIPS 3

The wrong side of the completed face should look like the photograph.

NECK 1

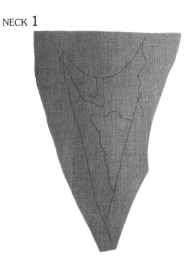

The next step is completing her neck. Trace the entire neck on to a piece of Number 1 fabric with at least 1" extra around the outside.

NECK 2

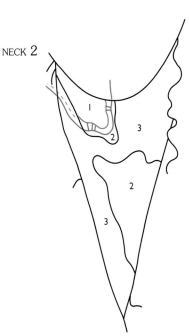

Place a piece of the Number 2 fabric cut the same size as the Number 1 fabric behind the work. Pin inside the Number 1 shape, and cut a seam allowance around the Number 1 shape; cut on the green lines as shown in the illustration and stitch on the red lines.

NECK 3

Return the work to the light box, realign the pattern and the fabric and redraw any lines that are missing on the Number 2 fabric. Turn to the wrong side and trim away any excess Number 2 fabric from under the Number 1.

NECK 4

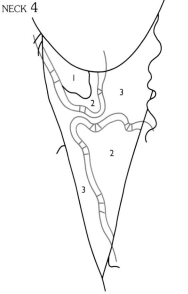

Cut a piece of the Number 3 skin fabric the same size as the first two pieces and place behind the work. Pin inside the Number 1 and 2 shapes along the lines where they join Number 3 shapes. Cut along the green lines as shown in the illustration and stitch along the red lines.

NECK 5

Return the work to the light box, realign the pattern and the fabric and redraw any lines that are missing on the Number 3 fabric.

Turn to the wrong side and trim away any excess Number 3 fabric from under the previous layers as shown in the photograph. The neck is now complete.

Trim the jaw line of the head to a seam allowance. Place the head on top of the neck, matching up the corresponding lines. Pin the head to the excess fabric of the neck and stitch in place.

Turn to the wrong side of the work and trim away the excess so it looks like the photograph.

The next step is making her clothing.

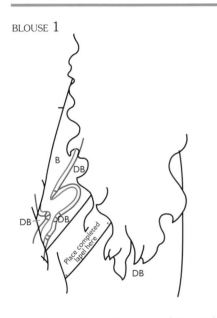

Trace the left lapel of the left side of her blouse onto the lighter shade of burgundy fabric (B). Cut it out with at least 1" of extra fabric all the way around. Cut a piece of the darker burgundy (DB) the same size and place it behind the first piece. Pin inside the B shapes where they join the DB shapes. Cut along the green lines and stitch along the red lines.

Turn to the wrong side and trim away excess DB fabric from under the B fabric. Return the work to the light box, realign the pattern and the fabric and redraw any lines that are missing on the DB fabric. Trace the remainder of the left side of the blouse onto the darker burgundy (DB) fabric and place the lapel where the seams join. Stitch the lapel in place. Trim excess fabric from behind the lapel. Cut the neckline edge of the left side blouse only, down to a seam allowance, pin on top of the neck and stitch in place. Turn to the wrong side and trim away the excess neck fabric from under the left side blouse.

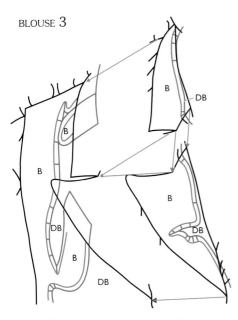

The right side of the blouse is worked the same way as the left side except that there are three separate sections: the upper lapel, the lower lapel, and the bodice. Work each section as you did for the left side blouse. Join the two lapel sections along their shared line, indicated by arrows.

Lay the lapel on top of the bodice and stitch in place.

Trim away any excess fabric from underneath as you complete each section and then join them together. Cut the neckline edge and front opening of the right side blouse to a seam allowance and lay it on top of the neck and left side blouse. Stitch in place and trim any excess fabric away from underneath the seam you have just completed. Trace the right arm on a piece of Number 1 fabric that's been cut the size of the arm plus 1" extra all the way around. Layer a piece of Number 3 fabric underneath and pin in the Number 1 shape along where it joins the Number 3. Cut the Number 1 shape with a seam allowance and stitch in place to the Number 3 fabric. Return the work to the light box, realign the pattern and the fabric and redraw any lines that are missing on the Number 3 fabric. The right arm is now complete.

Trim the outer edge of the right side of the blouse down to a seam allowance. Lay it over the right arm, matching the shared lines. Pin and stitch it in place. Trim excess arm fabric from underneath the blouse.

HAIR 1

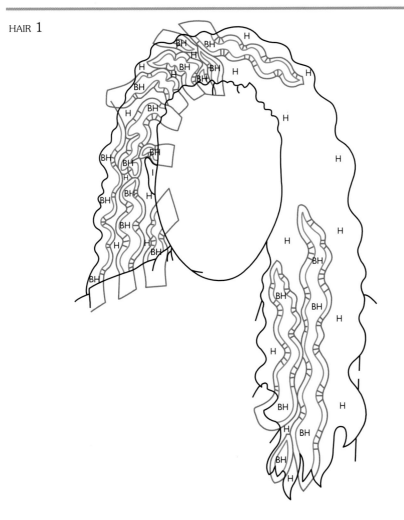

The next step is to make the hair. Trace the entire head of hair and an extra ½" of any lines from the face, neck, or blouse that intersect the brown hair fabric (BH). Cut the hair out with an extra 1" of fabric around the outside edges, leaving the center intact where the face will be placed. Cut a piece of the black hair fabric (H) the same size as brown hair fabric and layer it behind. Pin inside all the BH shapes. Cut narrow seam allowances and stitch along all the lines where BH and H join.

The photographs show the stitching of her hair in progress. Most of the BH shapes are too narrow to do any trimming from behind, but do it where you are able and most certainly behind the BH shape at the far right of the hair.

The right ear needs to be added on top of the fabric at this point. Trace the shape of the ear on the Number 1 skin fabric. Cut it out with a seam allowance all around except for the side that goes under the head, here an extra-wide allowance is left. Pin in place and stitch to hair, basting down the side which goes under the head. Trim the excess hair fabric from behind the ear.

Now trim all around the head and the right shoulder of the blouse down to a seam allowance. Lay the head and blouse on top of the hair and pin in place, matching the shared lines. Start at the * on the pattern and stitch only around the head and across the right shoulder. Trim away the excess hair fabrics from behind the head and make a clip to the * or knot (where you started stitching).

Now pull the left side of the hair over the top of the left side of the blouse. Pin and stitch in place. (Don't neglect the small crescent of dark burgundy between the left ringlets of her hair.) Trim away the excess neck and blouse fabric from behind the hair.

Trim the left side of the blouse and hair to a seam allowance. Trace the left arm onto a piece of Number 3 skin fabric. Cut it out with a seam allowance on the outside of the arm and an inch of allowance where it goes under the blouse and hair. Pin it in place, matching the shared lines and stitch the blouse and hair down to the left arm.

FIGURE 1

Trim away the excess arm fabric from behind the hair and blouse.

The figure of Samantha is now complete. Trim the remaining outer edges of the figure to a seam allowance as shown.

FIGURE 2

FIGURE 3

FIGURE 4

The wrong side of the work should look as shown (not terribly attractive from this side, is she?).

Pin the completed figure to a background (I used the back side of a print for mine) and stitch around the outside edges, matching thread as you work around the different fabrics.

Trim away the excess background fabric from behind the figure and the appliqué work for Samantha will be complete.

After working through one or more of these projects you should have a good idea of how the layering down process works and why it is more convenient and adaptable to making figures and faces. I can think of no other way of appliquéing in fabric that would lend itself so well to maintaining the integrity of a person's identity or leave you with a light fabric collage without any buildup of layers.

Cogitate

Perhaps after practicing the techniques on these projects you will be ready to try a face or figure that you have drawn. When working on your own project, the most important thing to remember is to take your time and think through each step of the project before actually doing it. I like the word "cogitate." It seems to imply more time and deliberation than mere thinking does. So cogitate before you cut, stitch, or baste. On my first project (Spacious Skies, page 6) I spent a lot of time staring at the pattern, staring at my fabrics, and planning out just what the results would be if I did such and such, and such and such, and such and such before I ever actually did the work. I did make mistakes every once in a while and had to backtrack and rework some things—just as anyone would have to if they were experimenting with new processes.

I don't have to cogitate as long with my projects as I used to because with my experiences behind me I pretty well know what I need to do and what the results will be. But that doesn't mean that I don't make mistakes. I still blunder now and then and have to backtrack. Don't get discouraged if you make mistakes—think of the errors as part of the learning process.

"It's only those who
do nothing that
make no mistakes,
I suppose."

Joseph Conrad

AIR SHOW, 1992, 81½" x 81½",
Jonathan Shannon. (Photo: R. Walker,
courtesy American Quilter's Society)
Jonathan wanted to create a
sense of movement and air and the way
the air holds the planes up.
Pinwheel blocks further the theme.

SHARING THE GOSSIP, 1994, 44½" x 44½", Heather Rose.
Inspiration for this quilt took shape while Heather was
having a cup of coffee and eavesdropping on waves of gossip.
People of different cultures and classes intermixing and
sharing secrets and news form layers like a quilt.

TRIBUTE, 1992, detail, Barbara E. Friedman.
The fluidity of modern dance is captured in this quilt
which evolved from photos in professional dance magazines.

AMIGOS MUERTOS, 1994, 89" x 89", Jonathan Shannon.
(Photo: S. Risedorph) The source for the imagery in this quilt
is the Mexican Day of the Dead. It is a time of spiritual closeness
for both the living and the dead. Jonathan writes, "I chose this
Mexican celebration as a memorial to all the artists who have died
from AIDS and cancer, and especially to my quiltmaker friend,
Lyn Piercy, who died as the quilt was being completed."

"The greatest use of
a life is to spend
it on something
that outlasts it."
William James

CHAPTER EIGHT

FAR AND NEAR LANDSCAPES

Up for Sure

While layering from the top down works wonderfully well for figures, it is not the way to construct a fabric landscape. We need to start layering with the part of the landscape that is furthest from view and then continuing the process by always working the layer that becomes the next furthest as you progress. Number the shapes on your paper pattern in the order of what is furthest away (like the sky) to what is the closest (the foreground); this order designates when each part of the scenery will be cut and sewn.

When making pictorial landscapes, many quilters start with a backing muslin. However, this means that all the pieces are placed and stitched onto the backing; then, the layers get stacked on top of each other and the layers also build up. It is difficult to make a nice, smooth top because the excess backing muslin can get in the way when trimming the layers.

Instead of using the muslin backing, I add a generous seam allowance to the pieces of fabric I am actually using for the appliqué. I trace the section on the light box, off of my pattern and onto my fabric, but I add the extra fabric to the traced edge. I add at least an inch of fabric around all the traced edges of the piece. Then when I lay the piece in place, I consider which seams will go on top of another piece or which seams will be going underneath another piece. The seams that go over another piece can be trimmed down to a regular ¼" seam allowance. For the seams that go under another piece, the extra allowance enables you to pin the next piece of appliqué on top of it and still have room to stitch. You will see how this works when you study the project in this chapter.

Appliqué work does tend to shrink a bit as the edges are sewn together, so it is important to give yourself extra fabric allowance on the edges of a quilt. This is imperative if you do want your quilt to be an exact measurement. For instance, if you are entering a contest that has a specified size requirement, or if you are planning to put a traditional pieced border around the quilt, you need to have the completed pictorial appliqué the size you intended. I generally leave at least 1" around the edges, more if it is a large quilt.

Keep your work flat while you are tracing the seam lines onto your fabric. While you are tracing, if the fabric is stretched or hangs off the edge of a table, your work could be distorted and you may end up with a top that ripples. If you are tracing a piece that is larger than your light box and the pattern and fabric must be draped over the box, you'll need to take certain precautions. Lay your pattern on a flat surface and pin (or tape using drafting tape) your fabric on top of the pattern. Then drape the pattern and fabric over the light box and move the project, if needed, until the whole section is traced.

I really have fun buying and using fabric for landscapes. I like to find the fabric that will give me a realistic portrayal of whatever it is that I am making—trees or flowering shrubs, sky, water, buildings, etc. These fabrics, if chosen with a discerning eye, can also give the illusion of details that I would have to otherwise create with smaller pieces of fabric. If you have not read about Fabric Choices in Chapter Four you may want to do so before starting a landscape.

Cape Elizabeth

I visited Cape Elizabeth a few years ago while teaching classes in Portland, Maine. It is a stunning place, landmarked by the Portland Head Light (a majestic lighthouse). I used one of my photographs to create this landscape project. Since I was limited by the size I could make this project, I eliminated many of the details of the actual scene. I drew up the pattern and then chose the fabrics as I constructed the project, pulling fabrics out of my stash as I came to that layer: sky, clouds, distant islands, sea, the lighthouse and surrounding buildings, rocks, shrubs, more shrubs, more rocks. I did not buy any fabric specifically for this project; I already had the fabrics. But, I make pictorial quilts so I naturally have these types of fabrics available. If you need to go out and buy fabric to make this project, consider the size of the section (an example is sky or water) and buy an appropriate amount.

You will need to trace the pattern from the tear-out at the back of the book on to another piece of white paper. This is so you can use the pattern on a light box without being confused by the pattern lines for the projects on the other side of the tear-out.

CLOUDS 1

Remember to start with the layer that is furthest from view. In this case, it is the sky. Using a removable marker trace the entire sky onto your chosen fabric. Include all the clouds, the horizon line with the shapes of the islands, and the part of the lighthouse above the horizon. Cut the fabric with an extra 1" allowance on all edges.

CLOUDS 2

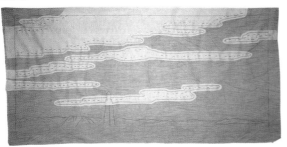

Trace the clouds onto your cloud fabric; you may trace each cloud separately to save material or you may draw them all at once just as you did with the sky. Take care to leave an extra 1" allowance on all the edges of the clouds that overlap the sides of the quilt. Cut a ¼" seam allowance for the edges of the clouds that are to be appliquéed on top of the sky fabric. Pin the clouds in place, matching any shared lines.

CLOUDS 3

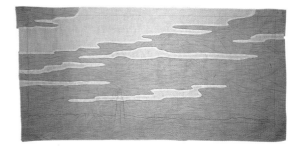

Stitch all the clouds in place starting ¼" outside the drawn edge of the quilt.

This is in case your appliqué shrinks as it is sewn together (it usually does).

CLOUDS 4

When the stitching of the clouds is complete, turn to the wrong side and trim away any excess sky fabric from behind the clouds.

103

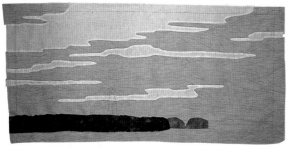

Next trace the two small islands and the strip of land that juts into the sea. I made the small islands a rather pale green because they are in the distance and in the mist. The strip of land is much greener because it is closer in view. Cut the regular ¼" seam allowance on the upper edge of these pieces and the generous 1" seam allowance on the lower edge; pin the pieces in place.

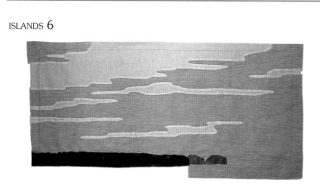

Stitch the upper edges only and baste the lower edges of island pieces in place.

Turn the work over and trim away the excess sky fabric from under the islands and strip of land.

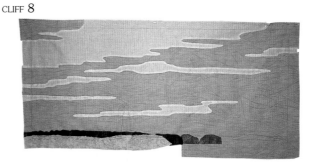

The next piece is the narrow strip of the cliff where the land meets the sea. Choose a pale, smaller-scale print of the fabric you intend to use for rocks in the foreground. Again, trace the shape, cut it with a regular ¼" seam allowance on the upper edge and a generous 1" seam allowance on the lower edge. Pin the piece in place.

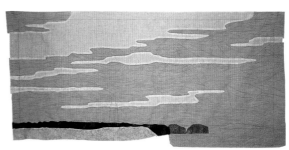

Stitch the upper edges only.

Turn the work over and trim away any excess green fabric from under the cliffs.

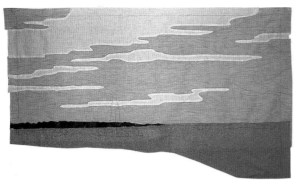

Work the sea next. Trace the shape—you may want to use a ruler to help you draw the horizon line straight—marking the lower edge of the large island and all the lines involved with both the far and the close shore, including the buildings where they cover the water.

The lighthouse breaks the land, cliffs, and water into two or three sections each. Notice that instead of cutting two pieces for the strip of land, and two pieces for the cliffs, and two pieces for the water, (which is what I would do if I wanted to make templates of everything) I just continue across as if there were nothing in front of the piece. This is a much easier way of constructing a landscape than dealing with several smaller pieces. I work this way when I am using the same piece of fabric if it continues across the landscape but it is broken up by objects in front of it. Stitch across the whole piece, but where another piece will cover the top of it, you can take bigger stitches and make a knot or backstitch just inside the seam line of the next piece.

Pin the sea piece in place, matching shared lines.

Stitch the sea in place.

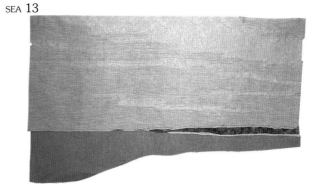

Turn the work over and trim away the excess sky, island, and cliff fabrics.

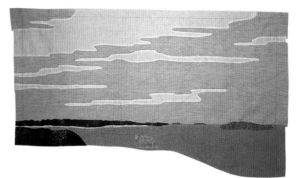

The next step is to add the shrubs behind the building, the rocks behind the retaining wall, and the large island pieces (Number 7, 8 and 9). Trace each piece onto an appropriate fabric. Cut the edges that will be appliquéed with ¼" seam allowances and cut an extra 1" allowance for the edges that will go under other pieces (the large island piece is appliquéed around the entire edge). Pin the pieces in place, matching shared lines.

Stitch the pieces in place and baste any loose vertical edges.

Turn the work over and trim away any excess fabric.

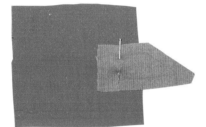

It is now time to construct the buildings and lighthouse. To do this, put the sides and roofs of the buildings together independently, aside from the background. (This will recall lessons learned in Chapter Seven where the layering is done working downward instead of upward.) Start with the building to the right of the lighthouse and select the two colors you will be using for the roof. Trace the lighter roof piece (Number 10) along with any intersecting lines. Cut a square of the darker roof fabric but do not make any markings on it at this time. Pin the lighter roof piece on top of the darker.

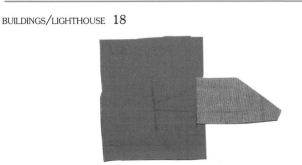

Stitch only on the line that joins the two pieces. Return to the light box, realign the two stitched pieces on top of the pattern and draw the lines for the piece (Number 11) onto the darker roof fabric. Trim away the excess dark fabric from under the light fabric.

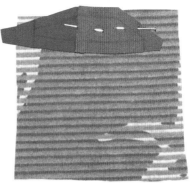

Pin the roof to a square of the fabric that you have selected for the darker side of the building. (I used a fabric that has palm leaves printed over stripes. I was able to use one part of the print for the lighter side of the building and another part for the dark.) Stitch the piece in place only where the roof joins that wall of the building. Return to the light box, realign the building on the pattern and draw the lines of the piece (Number 12) and any intersecting lines (notice there is a generous seam allowance on the lower edge of the building where it will go under the fence).

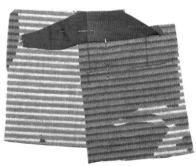

Trim away any excess striped fabric under the roof; trim the edge of the piece, where it joins the next piece (Number 13), down to a seam allowance. Pin a piece of the fabric you have selected for the next piece (Number 13) under the roof and wall. If you are using a striped fabric you will want to angle it slightly to show perspective.

Stitch across the edge of roof and down the wall where it joins the piece (Number 13). Return to the light box and draw in the missing lines.

Trim away the excess fabric from behind the wall and roof. This building is complete.

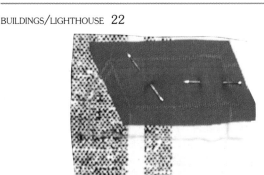

Work the building at the far left next (Number 14, 15a, 15b, 16). I used a striped fabric to simulate the darker wall and a doorway for this building. If you do not have a striped fabric that will work, you will have to put two different fabrics together as was done for the previous building; this is the reason for numbering the pieces 15a and 15b. On their selected fabrics, draw the lines for both the roof and the walls. Line the two pieces up, matching shared lines. Pin the pieces in place. Stitch only where the roof joins the walls.

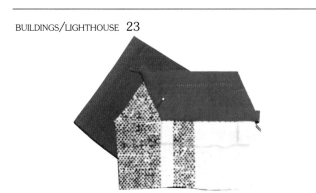

Pin a piece of the darker roof fabric for the far eaves under the building.

Stitch across the tiny area where the roof joins the eave and then down to where the wall joins the eave. Draw the roof line on the eave, and trim away any excess fabric from behind the roof and the wall. Trim all the edges except the lower edge (where it goes under a shrub) down to a seam allowance. This building is now complete.

The next building is made from pieces Number 17 and 18. Choose an appropriate fabric for each piece, first tracing the piece (Number 17) onto the fabric and then pinning it to the other fabric.

Stitch across the bottom of the roof leaving the points of the eaves free. Draw the walls of the next piece (Number 18), and then trim away any excess fabric from behind the roof and sides down to a seam allowance—leave a generous allowance at the lower edge. This building is now complete.

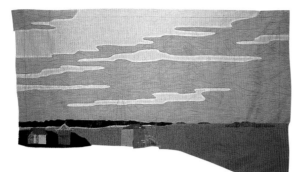

These three buildings may now be attached to the background fabric. Pin the pieces in place.

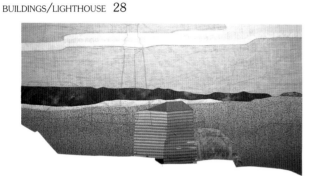

There should be outlines of the buildings on the background to show placement. The first building is stitched down along its far right wall and across the roof. Baste the edge where it goes under the lighthouse and the edge that's still loose.

Stitch the other two buildings around both walls and roofs. Baste the sides that have the generous allowance. Trim away any excess fabric from behind these buildings.

The lighthouse is next. Trace the main part of the lighthouse onto white fabric (Number 19). Cut the edge that joins the next piece (Number 20) to a seam allowance. Pin the piece to a rectangle of your selected gray fabric. Stitch along the edge where the two pieces join.

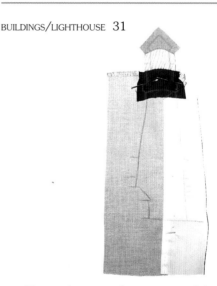

Trace the next three pieces (Number 21, 22, and 23) onto the selected fabrics. Stitch the pieces together where their lines join, laying Number 21 and 23 over Number 22. Pin this section to the top of the previous section (Number 19 and 20). Stitch along the adjoining line. Trim away any excess white and gray fabric, then trim all the sides, except the lower edge of the lighthouse, down to a seam allowance.

Pin the lighthouse in place, matching the lines drawn on the background. Stitch the pieces in place, basting the edges that go under the building and the edges at the base of the lighthouse. Trim away excess fabric from under the lighthouse.

Stitch the next pieces (Number 24 and 25) together, working as you did with first building. Leave the generous seam allowances where the edges will go under other pieces. Stitch and baste in place; trim any excess fabric from behind the pieces. Note the piece (Number 26) pinned to the piece that is selected for the roof (Number 27). Stitch along the lines that join the roof only. Stitch these pieces in place, basting down the generous seam allowances and trimming out the excess fabric from behind.

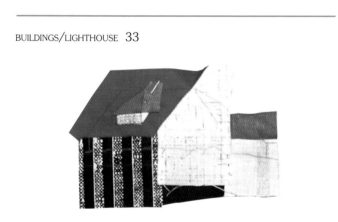

Construct the main building. Stitch the first three pieces together (Number 28 to Number 29a and 29b). Here I again used one piece of my striped fabric. Stitch piece Number 30 to 31 and then stitch the two to Number 32 (a-d). (I used the striped fabric again to simulate a columned porch.) Stitch the building (pieces Number 28 and 29 sewn together) onto piece Number 31. Trim away any excess fabric from behind while you are working these steps. Stitch piece Number 33 to 34 and then stitch those two pieces to Number 35a and 35b (more striped fabric here). Stitch that section on top of roof piece Number 30 except at the top roof line.

Trim away the excess roof fabric from under that section; trim all but the lower edge of the building to a seam allowance. Pin in place, matching to the placement lines on the background. Stitch in place around all the building's side and roof edges, except the lower edge. Baste any edges of the generous seam allowance together.

Turn to the wrong side and trim away any excess background fabric from behind the main building. All the buildings are complete.

Trace the next two pieces (Number 36 and 37) onto the selected fabric. (I chose a narrow stripe to simulate a picket fence). Cut the edges with ¼" seam allowance on the upper edge and sides, but keep a generous allowance on the bottom. Stitch the two pieces together where they join. Pin the pieces in place, matching shared lines.

Stitch the pieces in place. Trim the excess fabric from behind the fence. Trace, cut, pin, and stitch the retaining wall (Number 38) where it belongs and trim the excess fabric from behind.

All of the field (all Numbers 39) are traced showing placement of shrubs and rocks; cut as one piece. Pin the piece in place, matching shared lines. Stitch together where it meets the fence and retaining wall. Baste where it meets the rocks and water and below the building at the far left—this area will be covered by the next layer of rocks and shrubs. Trim away the excess fabric from under the field fabric.

Trace the rock piece (Number 40) onto the selected fabric. Cut the edges with a ¼" seam allowance, except where it goes under the upcoming pieces. Place a swatch of the fabric selected for Number 40a behind its outline on Number 40; reverse appliqué it to the piece. Turn to the wrong side and trim away any excess fabric from the piece (Number 40a). Pin the rocks on top of the field, matching any shared lines.

Stitch around all the rocks, basting the edges that go under the upcoming pieces.

Turn to the wrong side and trim the excess fabric from behind the rocks.

Trace the next three pieces (Number 41, 42 and 43) onto the selected fabrics; you can choose all the same fabrics or use different fabrics for each shrub—just make the texture or print slightly larger than the fabric used for piece Number 7 or Number 4. Cut the edges of the pieces with a ¼" seam allowance, except for Number 41 which has an edge that extends past the edge of the quilt. Pin the pieces in place, matching placement lines. Stitch the pieces in place. Trim the background from behind these pieces where possible.

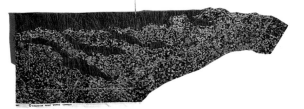

The pieces numbered 45 are supposed to be shadows in the shrubs. Choose a fabric for piece Number 44 that is larger in scale than any of the previous green pieces; choose a complementary darker fabric for the shadows. Pin a piece of the Number 45 fabric behind the Number 44 fabric, pinning all around the Number 45 shapes. Reverse appliqué the shadows into the shrubs.

Redraw any seam lines that are missing on the shadow pieces. Trim away the excess fabric around the Number 45 pieces. Trim the upper edge of the shrubs to a ¼" seam allowance. Pin these shrubs to the project, matching the shared lines along the field. Stitch the pieces in place. Trim away any excess field fabric from behind the shrubs.

Choose a large scale print for the rocks, such as one of Hoffmann's 3-D Prints. These rock shapes are constructed just like the shrubs in the previous stage except that there are two steps to the reverse appliqué. Trace all the rock lines (Number 46) on to the selected fabric. One set of the shadows (Number 47) is reverse appliquéd into the rocks with a piece of darker brown fabric pinned behind. Trim away all the excess Number 47 fabric from behind once the stitching is done for those shapes. The other set of shadows (Number 48) is reverse appliquéed into the rocks with a dark gray textured fabric pinned behind. Trim away all the excess Number 48 fabric when the stitching is done for those shapes. Redraw any lines that are missing on the Number 47 and 48 fabrics. Trim the upper edge of the rocks to a ¼" seam allowance.

Pin the rocks in place, matching the shared lines with previous sections.

Stitch along the rock line to complete the appliqué for Cape Elizabeth.

Turn the work over and trim away any excess fabric from behind the rocks. The wrong side of the finished piece is one layer of fabric except at the seam allowances. Everything you have learned in doing this small project is applicable to a landscape of much larger size.

"Friendship is unnecessary, like philosophy, like art… It has no survival value; rather it is one of those things that give value to survival."

C.S. Lewis

ICE CASTLE, 1990, 41" x 34", Audree Sells. Audree made the quilt in commemoration of the Minnesota Winter Festival.

SENTINELS, 1990, 94" x 46", Charlotte Warr Andersen.
(Photo: Ken Wagner Photography)
An Arizona sunset, strikingly created with vivid colors.
The sunset is all appliquéd by layering forward from
the pale yellow sky fabric, which is the furthest from
view. The border is pieced.

JORNADA DEL MUERTA, 1989, 96" x 36", Sandra Townsend Donabed.
Out of gas in a rental car in the desert, Sandra decided that
rather than yelling at her husband, she would commemorate
the incident with a quilt.

LONE CYPRESS, 1992, 37" x 47", Jan Clarke. (Photo: Thomas Anastasion Studio) Working from a friend's (Dorothy C. Harris) photograph, Jan created this lovely seascape.

CABIN IN THE WOODS, 1992, 18" x 24", Carol Meyer. (Photo: Thomas Anastasion Studio) Carol drew from nature and from an inspiring scene in Florida to make this quilt.

JOINED BY A RIVER, 1993, 58" x 36", Marlene Brown Woodfield. (Photo: Thomas Anastasion Studio) This is a contemporary charm quilt with each different appliqué piece made with a different fabric—359 in all!

BOUNDARY WATERS LEAVES #3:
AUTUMN MAPLES AND BIRCHES,
1990, 41" x 36", Carol Wagner.
(Photo: Thomas Anastasion Studio)
The last of a series, this quilt was
inspired by the high contrast of
yellow, gold, and copper leaves
against a deep sapphire sky.

FROM DEEP PLACES, 1994, 35"
diameter, Lura Schwartz Smith.
(Photo: Thomas Anastasion Studio)
A commissioned wedding gift,
this quilt combined the interests
of the Australian woman who
had a special love for the sea and
the Englishman of Greek heritage.
Some of the images were
photocopied and then screen-
printed from Lura's drawings, while
others she painted and then
appliquéd into the quilt.

"The great thing and
the hard thing is to
stick to things when
you have outlived
the first interest, and
not yet got the second
which comes with a
sort of mastery."

Janet Erskine Stuart
Life and Letters of Janet Erskine Stuart

CHAPTER NINE

CULMINATION

Alternatives

I feel that knowing which direction to layer opens a whole world of possibilities to the appliqué artist. You can portray anything within the limits of the fabric medium—I am always trying to push past those limits. One of my favorite mind games is trying to figure out how to portray something in fabric that I would likely think impossible. Mastery of the layering technique may switch on a proverbial light bulb over your head after trying only one of the projects. But don't be surprised if it takes much more experience than that. The methods I have recounted are time consuming and certainly none of them can come close to being called "speed" methods. I have been accused of being anal retentive more than once and I think of it as a backward compliment. It takes time to do something well and my quilts are nothing if not done well. But don't think that the only way to use the methods in this book are exactly this way or that you need to work in any specific order. I am not a dogmatic person and I will not tell you that it has to be done a certain way, and only that way, to make a wonderful quilt.

The quilting world is wide open and the boundaries of what make a great quilt are ever expanding. My purpose in writing this book is in hope that you like my quilts and are interested enough to read about and investigate the way I construct them. As you work through the techniques perhaps you'll find something you can apply to your quiltmaking. Or you may find something to help you portray your subject matter easier. Take what you like and makes sense to you, and use it! File the rest away in some little storage space in the back of your brain, or toss it out altogether. This is what the learning process is all about.

For example, Beth Kennedy makes remarkable and phantasmagorical quilts, and she has quite a reputation as a quiltmaker. She took my class because she had a project in mind where she wanted to achieve shaded depth and dimension in the quilt. I helped her draw up the pattern for her project, but she had no desire to work the appliqué by hand (that isn't her interest). Instead she took the pattern, cut all the shapes in fabric without seam allowances, and bonded them to a background. Then she machine stitched back and forth using matching thread with straight stitch embroidery to cover and "feather" the raw edges. This stitching was done after the quilt had its layer of batting and backing, so the quilting and edging were completed in one step. The quilt turned out beautifully and Beth won an Award of Merit at the 1992 AIQA Judged Show at the Houston International Quilt Festival.

Carol Goddu has a very different way of working. Her quilts are full of figures and she is currently working on a series of quilts with a dance theme. She used a number of techniques in her quilt, MOULIN ROUGE. This quilt is very dimensional, but it achieves that dimension by different means. Carol worked a narrow machine satin stitch using matching thread around the face and hair of each person. These shapes are not stitched to the background, but are made independently with their own filler and backing. Then they are hand stitched in place. The can-can dancers' legs are truly amazing. Each leg is

LES AMIS, 1992, 44" x 32", Beth Kennedy. (Photo: Thomas Anastasion Studio) A picture postcard from France was the inspiration for this quilt. It is one of Beth's quilt series devoted to matriarchal rituals.

MOULIN ROUGE, 1993, 58" x 72", Carol Goddu. (Photo: Thomas Anastasion Studio) Inspiration for this lively quilt was drawn from a variety of sources: photos, movies, line drawings. It is one of a continuing series of quilts on dance.

made with a front and back fabric stitched with a seam that you'd use for making a doll, with the leg turned inside out and shaped around some stiff substance so it is flat but still has body. Then the legs are covered with a sheer fabric to look like silk stockings. There is hand appliqué here and there to join the pieces. The dresses are made from a riot of ruffles and laces. You envision these ladies throwing their skirts out at you. The whole is a dazzling work and captures all the gaiety of that time and place.

I plan on combining my layering techniques with speedier machine techniques, just to see how it will work. I'll test some fusibles, check the look of the machine satin stitch, and perhaps try some machine blind-stitch appliqué. Those of you experienced in these techniques may have already figured out how to apply layering to your work.

Most people probably do not share my aversion to embroidery. When I taught at the Australian Quilt Symposium in Brisbane, it increased my exposure to embroidery. Australians seem to love embroidery as much or more than they do quiltmaking. They are extremely competent needle women and skillfully mesh their quilting and embroidery work. (They are such great needle women and quiltmakers that I found

MOUNT PLEASANT MINERS, 1992, 48" x 55",
Nancy S. Brown. (Photo: courtesy
American Quilter's Society) Made as a
tribute to Nancy's great-grandfather,
William Brown, who worked at the Mount
Pleasant mine for 17 years. The faces and
hands are hand-painted with fabric paint.

myself wondering why they went to the bother and expense of having us American quilt teachers "down under.") Several of the quilts shown in this book have more than just a touch of embroidery. I just tell myself, "When you gotta do it, you gotta do it."

Many artists are combining other media in their quilts. Nancy S. Brown's magnificent quilt, MOUNT PLEASANT MINERS, is such an example. Most of the fabrics in the quilt are hand-dyed or over-dyed which gives it a truly historic flavor. The quilt is not very big; the figures of the miners are relatively small. Their features would have been impossible to appliqué. The details of their faces and hands are painted on with fabric paint. This is an appropriate solution. The painting is skillfully done and blends in with the antique patina of the rest of the quilt.

Lura Schwartz Smith combines many different processes in her quilts: hand appliqué, painting, dye painting, soft sculpture, detail markers, screen print-

ing. She often makes line drawings (of her own ideas and designs, of course) and then transfers them to fabric by photocopying. ALL UP IN THE AIR is one of Lura's quilts where she used most of these techniques. Notice the lovely detail and dimension the photocopied lines add to the face and hands. After cutting out the photocopied shapes with a seam allowance, the shapes are then hand appliquéd in place.

ALL UP IN THE AIR, 1993, 34" x 32",
Lura Schwatrz Smith. (Photo: Thomas
Anastasion Studio) Lura writes, "I've always
loved white-face and juggling. But as I worked
on this piece of a woman juggling, I couldn't
help but to think of all the things a woman
must juggle: career, children, her spouse,
housework. What a trick it is to keep them up
in the air at all the same time." She uses
inking, painting, and other techniques to make
her quilts, as well as appliqué.

JULY, 1991, 91" x 103", Jonathan Shannon.
(Photo: DSI Studios, courtesy American Quilter's Society)
The imagery is inspired by a dream, so Jonathan set about
to create an illusion of space where things are both
different from reality yet still very believable.

Creative quilters are coming up with new techniques every day and I enjoy seeing the boundaries of our medium stretched. Some of the things we see are not particularly likable, but it is all part of the growth process that brings quilting into the realm of fine art. The following quote by Susan Sontag is applicable, "The purpose of art is always, ultimately, to give pleasure—though our sensibilities may take time to catch up with the forms of pleasure a given time may offer."

One famous artist that I am especially fond of is Salvador Dali. He and other artists like him brought us the world of surrealism. His paintings are full of recognizable, real objects. But the landscape he presents by combining the objects can not be found on this earth. In this vein, a quilt I particularly love is

Jonathan Shannon's JULY. This surrealistic dreamscape is cunningly wrought; we know fish and sunflowers do not dwell in the same environs; however, the images are beautifully executed and when combined in the quilt, they tell our senses we must be sleepwalking. Jonathan is not one of my former students. He has his own visions and techniques. I like to think, though, that my layering techniques would lend easily to surrealism. One could gather images from here and there, stitching each one independently, and then combine them to make a place that exists only in the mind. If you enjoy fantasy and science fiction literature like I do, it may open up whole "otherworlds" to paint with your fabric.

Assembling the Top

Once all the pictorial appliqué portions are complete, it is time to assemble the portions into a top. Of course, if you've only appliquéd a single figure or a landscape and hadn't planned on borders, then your work on the top is done. I have to say, though, that I like seeing borders of some sort on a quilt.

Several years ago, my local guild had a guest speaker. He was a framer who frames and finishes photos and artwork. He brought several examples of his work along, focusing mainly on needlework pieces. He had beautifully matted and elaborately framed the work, and was trying to recruit quilters who would let him frame their quilts. As well done as I thought he finished the pieces, I was somewhat put off by the whole idea of framing a quilt. Having to add something to my quilt after I had finished it seemed a bit of an insult, as if the statement I had made in my quilt was incomplete.

I see nothing wrong with matting and framing a piece of appliqué work. Many times after finishing a project I am tempted to just put it on stretcher bars and frame it. But I like entering my things in quilt shows and you can't enter them if they aren't quilted. Also, framing takes away from the fact that your work is a quilt. I am not talking about putting a quilt under a protective box, I am referring to actually flattening it under a glass and frame. I consider borders to be the frame for my quilts, even though at times I do not put a border on all sides of the work.

One of my favorite borders is to use traditional pieced quilt blocks that have a name that relates to the subject matter of my quilt. For the Olympic quilt shown on page 45 I went through my quilting books that illustrated traditional blocks. My favorite is Barbara Brackman's *Encyclopedia of Pieced Quilt Patterns* which has well over 4,000 blocks. When looking for blocks to use, I check the index of pattern names to find names that associate to my subject matter. Then I look up the pattern, seeing if I like how the pieces fit together while judging how it will look with the pictorial part of the quilt. If I choose it, I draft it to the required size and compose it in fabrics that mesh with the quilt. Some of the blocks I used for the Olympic quilt are Fair Play, Under Blue Mountain Skies, Gold & Silver or Winter Star, Hopes and Wishes, Shining Hour and Best of All—all names I thought were applicable to the spirit and purpose of the Olympics.

If you work beyond making the pictorial appliqué (by adding borders or combining with pieced blocks or other appliqué), it is very important to leave the generous seam allowances around all the outer edges of the quilt, as explained in Chapters Seven and Eight. Appliqué has a tendency to shrink as you stitch the pieces together. The denser and smaller the pieces the more it shrinks. The landscape I made of Cape Elizabeth stayed fairly true to size except where the buildings are located. That section is a conglomeration of small pieces so the quilt top pulled in quite a bit. I didn't worry because I had left the generous seam allowance around the entire outside of the project. It easily accommodated the size I originally planned for it and had plenty to spare when I trimmed the edges down to their appropriate seam allowance.

Collaging several different scenes or vignettes together may be something you want to try. I consider my quilt ...SO SHALL YE REAP to be my most ambitious yet. It consists of seven different vignettes that are separated by a pieced pattern loosely based on the old quilt pattern Periwinkle. I drew a full-size pattern for the quilt (it was a large piece of paper, 81" x 96") with all the piecing lines breaking the quilt up into its various scenes. I then drew the irregular shapes that made up the edges of each scene onto separate pieces of paper. Each vignette was individually drawn and then worked individually. I always left a generous seam allowance around the outside.

When all the appliqué was complete, I took the full-size paper pattern and cut it up into its sections, making a template for each of the vignettes. The lines were then traced onto the back side of each appliqué scene and the pieces cut with a ¼" seam allowance. The lines I traced on the right side of the appliqué,

...So Shall Ye Reap, 1993, 81" x 96", Charlotte Warr Andersen. (Photo: Borge Andersen & Associates) Commissioned by the LDS Church of History and Art as part of a sesquicentennial display for the Relief Society (the Church's women's organization). The quilt shows women in their daily righteous activities.

which show the edges of the piece, most often did not match those drawn on the back side. But it did not matter because I had given myself a generous seam allowance and had marked the fabric with a removable marker. The pieced pattern was then joined along the edges of the vignette, thus each scene was sewn to the next until the pictorial section of the quilt was together. I selected two traditional blocks for the borders of the quilts. Enigma is the name of the blocks across the bottom of the quilt and Guiding Star is fittingly across the top of the quilt.

Another challenging artwork is THE HERITAGE QUILT by the Chaska Heritage Quilters. This is a breathtakingly done quilt with vignettes that montage seamlessly from one to the next. I thought there would be no other way to make this quilt than to start with a generously cut, full-size background fabric and then place each of its figures, buildings, and other items onto it. However, Audree Sells, the director of the project, later told me that different people worked on different sections of the quilt. Additional appliqué was added to cover the seamlines where the sections were joined.

THE HERITAGE QUILT, 1988, 72" x 82", Heritage Quilter's of Chaska, Minnesota; Director of project: Audree Sells. This project was initiated by the Chaska Historical Society. The way the vignettes flow from one to the next is particularly attractive.

It was quite a feat to accomplish because more than 50 people worked on the quilt, and none formerly belonging to a quilt group.

Quilting

Once you've decided your appliqué is in need of quilting, you need to select a batting. Choose only very thin battings. The thicker battings add too much loft and distort the shapes you have worked so hard to maintain with your intricate stitching. There are two batts that I prefer above anything else I have tried. One is Mountain Mist Quilt Lite® which is thin and airy 100% polyester and the easiest of batts to actually quilt through. The other batt is Hobbs Thermore®. It is very thin and very flat yet adds lot of body to the quilt without adding puffiness. It is not as easy to quilt through as the Quilt Lite, but it is flatter than the Quilt Lite. If you want a super thin batt you can carefully split the Hobbs Thermore. I haven't tried this with a quilt, yet, but used the split batt on a quilted garment, which turned out very well.

Besides batting you will need a backing. I like to relate my backings to the front of the quilt by selecting one of the fabrics I used on the top. If you have lovely quilting stitches and want them to show on the back side, you will want to choose a solid fabric. If not, use a nice, busy print so those stitches will not be noticed. I try to make my backing a couple of inches larger than the top so I can encase the edges of the project while I'm quilting.

I have a traditional type quilting frame that has boards of adjustable sizes that are C-clamped together at the corners. I stretch my backing, batting, and top in the frame using thumb tacks, measuring the sides and across the diagonal of the quilt from opposite corners to make sure my quilt is square or rectangular. I then use a 3" soft sculpture doll needle and a cone of white thread to baste the quilt together. I cross-hatch the whole quilt, taking stitches that are at least an inch long and rows that are 3" apart. Cross-hatching means the rows run both up and down, and side to side on the quilt. When the quilt is taken out of the frame, I fold the excess backing fabric to the front of the quilt to encase the batting and baste the folds down. I am ready to quilt at this point.

Quilting in a hoop is the method that seems to work best for me. I need the tension that the stretching action of a hoop or frame creates to get my stitches to look right. My friends, Jeana Kimball and Joan Rollins are both lap quilters. They prepare the quilt just like I do to the point where it's basted and taken out of the frame. But then they do all their quilting with the quilt bunched up in their lap—without a hoop or frame. They both have beautiful quilting stitches, in fact Jeana's stitches look just like mine. I did some quilting on one of her pieces when she had a deadline closing in. I had to use my hoop, of course. It was very hard to tell where her stitches ended and mine began. So use the method that suits you the best and gives you the best results.

I used to quilt in a frame but found that it was very hard on my back (all those hours spent crouched in the necessary position). With my hoop, I can wriggle down into a corner of my sofa and pull my hoop back to me. With added back support I can quilt for hours.

Notice I have not mentioned anything about marking quilting lines. It is at this point—when I have my project layered, basted and stretched in a hoop—that I worry about where I am going to quilt. I usually do my outline (or stitch-in-the-ditch) quilting first as the lines I am quilting are already there and require no marking. I feel that outline stitching is the only type that should be done on a face or other body parts unless you want to add wrinkles, scars, or smile lines to the skin. (A reason why I design my appliqué so the pieces are not too big and the quilting lines are close enough and adequate for the batting.)

Outline quilting for the face

More quilting lines are added to texturize hair.

When I am outline quilting I try to get as close to the seam line as possible. Even though my quilting stitches look pretty good, I do not want them to show that much or distract from the appliqué. This applies mainly to figures, mind you, and for this outline quilting I use a matching thread. I like using quilting thread for quilting. Spools of thread that are meant to be used for quilting will say "quilting" somewhere on them. However, the number of colors and shades of quilting thread is limited—often you can't match the thread to the fabric that needs the outline quilting. I would rather have my thread match than use a quilting thread, so I substitute with a cotton-covered polyester thread. I do not believe you should use a 100% cotton *sewing* thread for quilting: it is not strong enough. All this means I will have many colors of threads showing on the back side of my quilt. Some people believe that quilt show judges will give you negative marks if you use more than one color of quilting thread. This is an incorrect myth. What counts is if what you have used and where you have used it is right for the quilt.

Once the outline quilting is complete, I decide what textures and designs I want to add. I do want these quilting lines to show. If I have a cloud shape I may want to add puffy rounded lines. Bushes and trees may need ruffled and meandering lines. A person's hair is a great place to add lots of quilting lines and using different colors may add a streaky look. Bricks can be quilted into sides of buildings, feathers on to birds, ripples into water, and wrinkles or folds into clothing.

Even though it is my least favorite stage of making a quilt, I have always put a lot of hand quilting in my quilts. I don't like doing it, but I love seeing it completed. All those minuscule hills and valleys, the ridges, the hints of texture created by those thousands, perhaps millions, of stitches are what I love about the finished surface of a quilt.

I mark my quilting lines as I go with a Dixon Washout Cloth marker. I work a section at a time, stretching it in a hoop and marking the appropriate lines. Most of the time I mark these lines freehand since they are intended to make natural textures. I do use stencils or templates occasionally, again marking while the quilt is in the hoop.

My original intention was to machine quilt NAIAD (page 49). However, too many of my friends said it would be a sin to use machine stitching on top of all that hand appliqué. I have no objection to machine quilting when it is done well, but I have little experience with it. Maybe one day I'll be competent enough to master quilting with a machine.

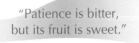

"Patience is bitter,
but its fruit is sweet."

Lida Clarkson
Brush Studies in *Ladies' Home Journal*

Quilting Textures

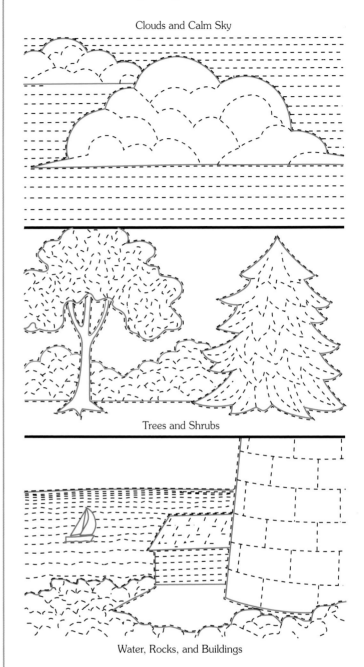

Clouds and Calm Sky

Trees and Shrubs

Water, Rocks, and Buildings

Finishing

The way my mother taught me to finish a quilt was to trim the back and the top evenly, turn in a ¼" seam on both, and then slip stitch or ladder stitch the edges together along the two folds. I learned the hard way that this was not an acceptable edge for a quilt. I took one of my quilts to sell at a consignment shop and was told in no uncertain terms that it was not a proper way to finish a quilt.

I have been putting bindings on my quilts ever since and almost all the bindings I make are on the bias. I have judged several quilt shows and the bias bindings are always the ones that match the description of a well done binding. Most people seem to prefer the double bias binding. It makes a sturdy and durable edge for a quilt. But, hey! Most of the pictorial quilts we're discussing are intended to be hung on walls. Wall hangings don't have to submit to the endurance testing that bed quilts do. Here is a radical idea: wall hangings don't need bindings. But then, maybe it's not such a radical idea. Lately, I have seen quilts at shows that have the finish my mother taught me, and what's more, they have ribbons on them!

I have put piped edges on a few of my quilts. Piping makes an impressive finish and is fairly sturdy. But it all comes back to doing what's right for the quilt. A simple, non-distracting finish may be what is needed. You may choose a straight binding instead of a bias one to take advantage of a print or pattern in a fabric. Or the quilt may require some sort of elaborately sculptured edge. You are the artist—let the quilt speak to you and tell you what is best.

Don't forget to sign and label the quilt. The first few quilts I made (they were traditional ones that I sold at consignment shops) had no sort of label or signature on them at all. Somewhere out there, two people have quilts I've made (if they've taken care of them) but have no way of knowing it. Probably they could care less. I didn't know better at the time. I hadn't been instructed on quilt history and preservation, but it bothers me that I let those go without taking pictures of them or including some hint of their history. Now all the quilts I make have my initials in the lower right hand corner of the quilt front and a detailed label on the lower left back corner. I include at least my name, the date, and place it was completed, in addition to whom it was made for, and a few lines about the statement the quilt is meant to make. I make a smaller label with my name, address, and telephone number that I attach to the quilt to facilitate locating it should it be lost during shipping.

Make sure to take pictures of all your quilts, too. I might not even be able to recognize those unsigned quilts were I ever to see them again. Pictures definitely would have helped and been some testament to the fact I made those lost quilts.

I hope you find this book useful. If you've made a quilt that makes you proud as a peacock, and you've used some of the techniques in this book, I'd love to see a picture of it. I'm always on the prowl for pictorial quilts to freshen up my lectures and classes.

"Pay no attention to
what the critics say;
no statue has ever
been put up to a critic."

Jean Sibelius (attributed)

POSTSCRIPT

The techniques I have laid out in this book are not easy. I will not say they are not for beginners though, because some beginners have more stitching acumen than others. Some of the quilters whose works are included in this book considered themselves beginners.

I believe too many people set too low expectations for themselves. I always have high expectations of my students and take them on a little tougher road than they imagined they would take. Push yourself past what you think are your limits. It's the only way you'll grow and develop talent and surpass what you've done before.

I cannot help you any more with your tracing and drawing skills than what I've already explained in this book. You need to cultivate your own style of pictorial quilts. But I can give you one last stitching challenge, though. On the tear-out sheet at the back of the book, I've included the pattern for the face of my daughter, Aubry. There are no instructions included for the layering process or stitching her together. If you can make this face and have it turn out reasonably well, you will know that you have gained the insight I intended you to acquire through these pages. I hope that you will make use of your new skills and create some beautiful, pictorial appliqué works of your own.

ABOUT THE AUTHOR

Trailing a long background in the needlearts passed to her by her mother and grandmother, Charlotte Warr Andersen began making her first quilt (a Log Cabin) in 1974. Though immediately enchanted with the disciplines and pleasures involved in quiltmaking, she only made a few traditional quilts. It wasn't until Charlotte realized the possibilities of combining pictorial appliqué with traditional quiltmaking skills that she became a truly passionate quilter.

The competitive side of quiltmaking has an appeal for Charlotte. She has entered many of the biggest and most prestigious quilt shows and has often been successful. Her awards include second place in the first Great American Quilt contest in New York City, several first places at the American Quilter's Society show in Paducah, Kentucky, grand prize for the "Quilt a Modern Day Fairy Tale," contest in Odense, Denmark, and two Best of Show awards at the International Quilt Festival in Houston, Texas. Many of her quilts reside in museums and private collections.

A native of Salt Lake City, Utah, Charlotte resides with her husband, Eskild, four children, Amity, Dylan, Aubry, and Davyn, and a faithful dog, Betsy. She loves natural wonders, the outdoors, and open spaces, and is a member of the Nature Conservancy. When she is not quilting, along with traveling, teaching, or fussing over her four teenagers, Charlotte spends time reading fantasy and science fiction literature, and listening to alternative music.

If you are interested in Charlotte's workshop on Appliqué for Realism, or any of her other classes or lectures, write to her at 5740 Wilderland Lane, Salt Lake City, UT, 84118

Supply/Source List

Alpha Numeric Paper:
Summit Sales, 415 Regal Row, Dallas, Texas 75247
(214)637-0308

Opaque Projectors:
Artograph, 2838 Vicksburg Lane N., Plymouth,
Minnesota 55447 (800)328-4653
(Call for a brochure listing dealerships.)

Hand-dyed Fabric:
Lunn Fabrics, 357 Santa Fe Drive,
Denver, Colorado 80223 (303)623-2710
(shades, dye runs, air-brushed fabrics)

Skydyes, 83 Richmond Lane, West Hartford,
Connecticut 06117 (203)232-1429
(hand-painted cottons and silks)

Dyes:
Pro Chemical & Dye, Inc., P.O. Box 14, Somerset,
Massachusetts 02726 (508)676-3838

Light Boxes:
Seattle Woodworks, Limited, 13032 Robinhood Lane,
Snohomish, Washington 98290-3634 (206)794-8477
or (800)357-9663

Officemax stores nationwide—call (800)788-8080 to
find store location near you

Dixon Washout Cloth Markers:
Clotilde, 2 Sew Smart Way B8031, Stevens Point,
Wisconsin 54481-8031 (800)772-2891

Straw Needles and ¾" Extra Sharp Appliqué Pins:
Foxglove Cottage, P.O. Box 18294,
Salt Lake City, Utah 84118

Bibliography

Andorka, Frank H. *A Practical Guide to Copyrights and Trademarks*. New York: World Almanac, an imprint of Pharos Book, 1989

Brackman, Barbara. *An Encylopedia of Pieced Quilt Patterns*. Lawrence, KS: Prairie Flowers Publications, 1979 (I), 1980 (II, III, IV), 1981 (V, VI), 1982 (VIII), 1983 (VII)

Buskirk. "Art and the Law, Appropriation Under the Gun," *Art in America*, June 1992, p.37

Conner, Karlen, Perwin, & Spatt. *The Artist's Friendly Legal Guide*. Cincinatti, OH: North Light Books, 1988

Crawford, Tad. *Legal Guide for the Visual Artist*. New York: Allworth Press, 1995

McKim, Ruby. *101 Patchwork Patterns*. New York: Dover Publications, 1962

Morris. "When Artists Use Photographs," *Artnews*, Jan 1981, pp. 102-106

Pinkerton and Guardalabene. *The Art Law Primer*. New York: Nick Lyons Book, 1988

Strong, William S. *The Copyright Book*. Cambridge, MA: MIT Press, 1993

Tescher, Judy Mercer. *Dyeing and Overdyeing of Cotton Fabrics*. Paducah, KY: Collector Books, Division of Schroeder Publishing, 1990

UNESCO, *The ABC of Copyright*. United Nations Educational, Scientific, and Cultural Organization, 1981, 1983; second impression, France

Wolfrom, Joen. *The Magical Effects of Color*. Martinez, CA: C&T Publishing, 1992

For more information write for a free catalog from:
C & T Publishing
P.O. Box 1456
Lafayette, CA 94549
(1-800-284-1114)